THE FISHING HERE IS GREAT!

THE FISHING HERE IS GREAT!

A light-hearted discourse on the social history
of angling as depicted on old postcards

Derek Mills

WILLOW BOOKS
Collins
8 Grafton Street, London W1
1985

To 'Henery',
from whom I learnt
that there was far more
to fishing than
catching fish

Willow Books
William Collins Sons & Co Ltd
London . Glasgow . Sydney . Auckland
Toronto . Johannesburg

British Library Cataloguing in Publication Data

Mills, Derek
    The fishing here is great –
    1. Fishing – History
    I. Title
    799.1'2'09   SH421

ISBN 0-00-218177-0

Set in Garamond
by Cheney & Sons Ltd.
Printed and bound in Great Britain by
William Collins Sons & Co Ltd, Glasgow

CONTENTS

Acknowledgements

I should like to express my gratitude to Raphael Tuck & Sons and Valentines of Dundee for their generous permission to reproduce so many of their cards in this book. My sincere thanks are also due to the following for allowing me to use their cards: Bamforth & Co; Colin Branch Wholesale, Rotorua, New Zealand; E.T.W. Dennis & Sons; Rudolf Georgi, Aachen, West Germany; Arthur Guinness & Sons; Lawson Graphics Atlantic, Halifax, Canada; MM-Verlag, Salzburg, Austria; Fjóla Sigmundsdottir, Reykjavik, Iceland; Smith-Western Inc, Portland, USA and Alex Wilson Coldstream Ltd, Dryden, Canada.

My acknowledgements are also due to the following for so kindly allowing me to reproduce extracts from their books: Jonathan Cape (*Rod and Line* by Arthur Ransome); Chatto & Windus (*My Moby Dick* by William Humphry); Douglas & McIntyre (*Bright Waters, Bright Fish* by Roderick Haig-Brown); Daniel Farson (*Going Fishing* by Negley Farson); Richard Gordon and William Heinemann (*Instant Fishing* by Richard Gordon); Dr Loren Grey (*Tales of Fishes* by Zane Grey); Robin Bruce Lockhart (*My Rod, My Comfort* by Robert Bruce Lockhart) and the Rt Hon The Lord Tweedsmuir (*Scholar Gypsies* and *Great Hours in Sport* by John Buchan).

Special thanks go to Mr Ron Coleby for searching the angling literature for women authors; Mr H. Richardson of *Transy News* for encouraging my card collecting activities, and to Mr Thor Gudjonsson of Reykjavik and Mr K. Larusson of the Iceland Tourist Board for arranging for me to use the three Icelandic cards.

INTRODUCTION

There are well over three and a half million anglers in the United Kingdom at present and, with increasing leisure time, this figure will continue to rise; that is if the anti-blood-sports lobby doesn't achieve its aims of having fishing banned along with hunting and shooting. That such a situation should come to pass seems unlikely, as fishing is enjoyed by all sectors of our democratic community. Such a threat to a long-established pastime is unlikely to go unchallenged and would be resisted equally by miner, clerk, lawyer, doctor, busdriver, farmer, shopkeeper and politician. It has attracted famous men of many nationalities ranging from Sir John Hawkins, Richard Sheridan, Charles Kingsley, Sir Humphry Davy, Arthur Ransome, Neville Chamberlain, John Buchan and Lord Home to Bing Crosby, Lenin and Chekhov. To be fair, there have also been some famous men who detested angling. Lord Byron denounced Izaak Walton as a quaint old coxcomb and considered fishing as the 'cruelest, the coldest and stupidest of sports'. Plutarch, in his book *de soler animal* speaks against all fishing as a 'filthy, base, illiberal employment, having neither wit nor perspicacity in it, nor worth the labour', while Robert Louis Stevenson began as an enthusiast but after catching three dozen trout one day 'forthwith forswore fishing' before he had reached the age of twenty-one.

We can read what some men say against our sport in an essay by Leigh Hunt or we can listen to the following verse addressed to a trout:

> So mayst thou live, O little fish;
> And if an angler for a dish,
> Thro' gluttony's vile sin,
> Attempts, a wretch, to pull thee out,
> God grant thee strength, thou gentle trout,
> To pull the raskall in.

But we can shake our heads with pity that such men should regard fishing with a blinkered eye and consider it only a contest between man and fish. There is no doubt that angling, like many sports, should have a code of honour, like the oath of Hippocrates in medicine. Perhaps this code has been lost in the upsurge of popularity and the rise in new participants.

So a pause to reflect and for a backward glance at our forebears' enjoyment of the Art is perhaps worthwhile. We can of course do this by looking at the literature on the subject, but our parents, grandparents, great-grandparents and great-great-grandparents unintentionally left us a more revealing record – a pictorial chronicle portrayed on postcards. Bless their happy souls, they used to send postcards as readily in those days as we nowadays pick up the telephone. The postal service was not overburdened and took a pride in prompt delivery. So a card sent on one day would predictably reach the addressee on the next, and it cost the sender only a halfpenny, or 0.208 new pence. Furthermore, the urge to collect was common and indulged with enthusiasm. Postcards were a cheap, accessible and collectable commodity within the reach of Everyman. There was no television to distract young Henry and his elder sister or old Aunt Maud from putting their card collections into ornate albums on a confined Sunday afternoon, or in an evening to the accompaniment of the wireless, if there *was* one in the house. Before 1922 there would not even have been that luxury and self-made amusement would have been the order of the day. The popularity of postcards seems to have been before that time and from 1900 to 1910 between one and three million postcards passed through the post each day. Cards covered every conceivable subject and fishing was one which was portrayed in all its aspects – romantic and humorous. Many of these cards have come my way and they depict a social history of the sport which no literature review can equal.

The following comment made by Miss Margaret Mead in the *Girl's Realm* in December 1900 leaves us in no doubt as to the future value of the picture postcard in tracing the social history of many subjects:

The picture postcard is a sign of the times. It belongs to a period peopled by a hurried generation which has not many minutes to spare for writing to friends. . . . The picture postcard is with us. It suits us. It meets our needs. I can imagine a future generation building up by their help all the life of today – our children, our pets, our adventurous youths, our famous old people, our wild and garden flowers, our outdoor delights, our life of sport, and our life of stress and strain; our national holidays, our Pageants, and traces of the drama of political life, are all to be found thereon.

So let us look at our angling past to help us guide its future and, as Neil Munro said:

> I must be rising and I must be going
> On the roads of magic that stretch afar,
> By the random rivers so finely flowing
> And under the restless star.

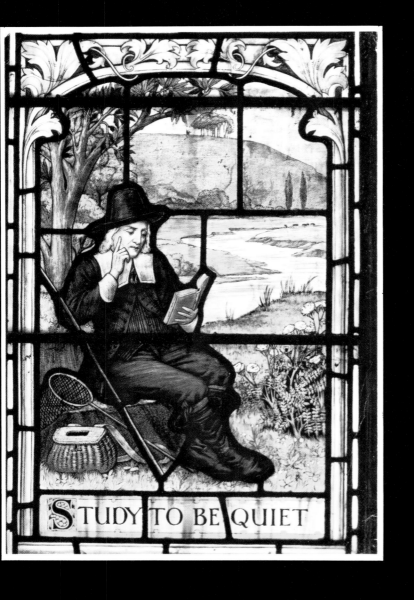
STUDY TO BE QUIET

Why Do We Go Fishing?

If you want to be happy for a day, get drunk.
If you want to be happy for a week, get married.
If you want to be happy for life, take up fishing.

Richard Gordon, *Instant Fishing*

Man has been fishing for sport for literally hundred of years. There are references to angling in the writings of Homer (*The Odyssey*), Theocritus, Plato (*Laws*), Pliny, Cicero and Herodotus as well as in many other Greek and Latin works. John MacDonald in his fascinating book *The Origins of Angling* refers to a funereal epigram of Sappho's, written about bc 600, which has long been accepted by fishing historians as the key to the old writing on fishing. Since those early years man has had considerable enjoyment from fishing and there is a considerable literature on the sport describing the exploits of man in pursuit of his quarry. However, over the last twenty years or so there has been a certain amount of heart-searching for an explanation of why we go fishing and how we can justify participation in what has come to be described by extremists as one of the 'blood sports'. This has resulted in a series of national surveys to measure the degree of participation in angling amongst the public in the United Kingdom and USA. One of the facets studied was 'motivation'. Why *do* people fish? It was not at all surprising to find that one of the reasons was the therapeutic benefits of the sport even though, as the Medway Report of 1980 stated, it caused some pain to the quarry. Do the therapeutic benefits outweigh the 'cruelty' effects? Some organisations such as the Society for the Prevention of Cruelty by Angling, the Animal Liberation Front and the Hunt Saboteurs' Association would say 'no'. But the Medway Panel, sponsored by the RSPCA, consider that the level of 'cruelty' can be reduced to an acceptable level if certain codes of practice concerning the type of fishing tackle used are observed.

1. A peaceful picture of contentment – suitable for the sitting room, study or office. Quite a good idea to take a book with you when you are fishing, it whiles away the time if the fish are not being co-operative; very good when going after sea trout at night – when you can no longer read you know it's time to start fishing! This stained-glass window depicting Izaak Walton is to be found in Winchester Cathedral.

2. Facsimile, with Transcript, of the first printed text of *The Treatise of Fishing with an Angle* (from the second *Book of St Albans*, 1496): 'Solomon in his proverbs says that a good spirit makes a flowering age, that is, a fair age and a long one. And since it is so, I ask this question, "What are the means and causes that lead a man into a merry spirit?" Truly, in my best judgement, it seems that they are good sports and honest games in which a man takes pleasure without any repentance afterward. Thence it follows that good recreations and honourable pastimes are the cause of a man's fair old age and long life. And therefore I will now choose any four good sports and honourable games, that is to wit: hunting, hawking, fishing and fowling. The best in my simple judgement is fishing, called angling, with a rod and a line and a hook.'

Here begynnyth the treatyse of fysshynge wyth an Angle.

Salamon in his parablys sayth that a good spyryte makyth a flourynge aege; that is a fayre aege & a longe. And syth it is soo: I aske this questyon. Whiche ben the meanes & the causes that enduce a man in to a mery spyryte. Truly to my beste dyscrecōn it semeth good dysportes & honest gamys in whom a man Joyeth Wythout ony repentannce after. Thenne foloWyth it þ goode dysportes & honest games ben cause of mannys fayr aege & longe life. And therfore noW Woll I chose of foure good dysportes & honeste gamys; that is to Wyte: of huntynge: haWkynge: fysshynge: & foulynge. The beste to my symple dyscrecōn Whyche is fysshynge: callyd Anglynge Wyth a rodde: and a lyne

AIN'T NEVER SEEN A MAN WHO COULD FISH AND WORRY AT THE SAME TIME!

3. Obviously a 'saying' that should be hanging over every angler's bed or, if his wife forbids it, in his 'den', shed or wherever he goes in the house for peace and quiet.

4. The 'contemplative angler' – many folk go fishing to get inspiration to write books, invest money and decide on marriage. This fellow's mind is more on liquid refreshment. A postcard of 1904 sent by a schoolgirl driven 'dotty' with term exams.

There is no doubt that angling is of immense value to the economy of many countries. It is also a very satisfying recreation and in one angling survey the different 'satisfactions' were given an order of ranking. The three with the highest ranking for anglers in general, and in order of importance, were (i) adventure and excitement; (ii) uncertainty: a lot of unexpected things can happen; and (iii) peace of mind and, coming third equal, the chance to be alone in a quiet, peaceful spot. The last had the highest ranking with coarse fish anglers, came second with game fishermen and fifth with sea anglers. Sea anglers put the highest value on the uncertainty involved.

Sir Robert Bruce Lockhart in his book *My Rod, My Comfort* felt that the desire for solitude is the most pleasant disorder of our times. It is man's natural reaction to the speed of modern life and to the evils of the

6. The 'uncertainty' involved in fishing or 'incerti della pesca' as the Italians say. This postcard was sent to someone in Scotland from Romania in 1905. The sender's appropriate comments are on the picture – 'ahem' – any minute now and the angler is going to be separated from his lunch.

5. Early evidence of fly-fishing in Germany in the thirteenth and fourteenth century comes from the Manesse Manuscript. Adoration is in the eyes of the onlooker (see Chapter 4).

world in which we live. And because today solitude is almost beyond our reach we seek it the more eagerly. Some find it only in dreams; others again on the mountain tops. The more fortunate satisfy their craving by the side of running streams and lonely lochs.

Fishermen are the same the whole world over it would seem and in a national household survey in the USA 68 per cent of the fishermen gave as their main reason for fishing that it relieved their tensions; the next important reason (51 per cent) being an escape from pressures of work. In a later survey by social scientists of Missouri trout anglers' attitudes to angling, it was found that the five most important reasons for fishing were relaxation, enjoyment of nature, to catch at least one trout, escaping daily routine and pressure of work. In a report on *Angling in Britain 1980* the Travis Commission felt that fishermen have a better chance of getting

7. *Thursday* by W. Dendy Sadler. This painting in the Tate Gallery shows an essential break from monastic duties to obtain fish for the monastery's Friday lunch. It looks as though a big carp is being brought to net.

8. Izaak Walton and Charles Cotton Fishing House, Hartington station. Issued by the London & North Western Railway Company who advise the reader on the reverse that it 'is noted for Punctuality, Speed, Smooth Riding, Dustless Tracks, Safety and Comfort, and is the Oldest Established Firm in the Railway Passenger Business.' Postmark 1909.

9. A man with the right idea, but he could have kept his beer cooler if he'd suspended it in the water. A 1914 postcard by the popular postcard artist 'Comicus'.

through life without a mental breakdown than non-anglers. One thing seems certain – the majority of fishermen agree with the thoughts of one of Izaak Walton's friends who had this to say in *The Compleat Angler*:

. . . angling was, after a tedious study, a rest to his mind, a clearer of his spirits, a diverter of sadness, a calmer of unquiet thoughts, a moderator of passions, a procurer of contentedness, and . . . it begat habits of peace and patience in those who professed and practised it.

A poem by the Master of angling reinforces this feeling:

Let me live harmlessly, and near the brink
Of Trent or Avon have a dwelling-place,
Where I may see my quill or cork down sink,
With eager bit of Perch, or Bleak, or Dace,
And on the world and my creator think;
Whilst some men strive ill-gotten goods t'embrace,
And others spend their time in base excess
Of wine, or worse, in war and wantoness.

Two hundred years later the *Encyclopaedia of Rural Sports* considered that:

Angling as an amusement presents features of great attraction: it is far from dangerous and explosive, but on the contrary is productive of interest and amusement without any great pecuniary sacrifice. Its apparent simplicity allures many into the practice . . . he [the angler] soon discovers that extreme nicety and precision, great patience, caution and perseverance, are essential to the attainment of proficiency in the art. . . .

8

ISAAC WALTON & CHARLES COTTON FISHING HOUSE — L & N.W. RAILWAY.

9

"No boss, I don't catch many fish, but it passes the time, and keeps a man out o' the pubs!"

"PATIENCE ON A MONUMENT."

10

The "BAND OF HOPE"

WANSTEAD PARK

11

"Now then John, move up"

Angling is a great leveller of all men. Fish do not distinguish between sex, creed, race or political affiliation. There are a number of great politicians in the angling hall of fame, but perhaps more should cultivate the gentle art because, as Izaak Walton said, 'We anglers all love one another.'

Judging by the number of postcards on the subject, drink seems to figure prominently in the gentle art. Perhaps one of the reasons we go angling is to keep away from the pubs, not to avoid alcohol of course, but to drink it in more idyllic surroundings and while away long fishless hours.

The element of uncertainty which many fishermen desire can manifest itself in many ways. Some of them can be most unpredictable – an unexpectedly large fish, an amorous affair or a minor disaster. According to Arthur Ransome half the pleasure of fishing comes from the uncertainty of one's reaction to that sudden crystallization of emotions held as it were in suspense. If there were no surprise at all one could count on oneself and hook one's fish with almost mechanical certainty and, having got so far, one would give up fishing and look for something more exciting.

Most anglers consider uncertainty in a rewarding way, namely the ever-present chance of landing a big fish. Hence *The Angler's Prayer*:

13. The word 'Hope' appears again – with the angler hoping for a fish to take his bait. Being an optimist enables one to put up with all forms of inclement weather!

14. 'We anglers love one another.' This situation does arise occasionally but it's usually resolved amicably and with some amusement, but unlikely in this instance – probably from different clans.

13

Lord give me grace
to catch a fish
So large that even I,
when talking of it
afterwards,
May never need to lie

There is another poem, *The Fisher*, which also portrays his thoughts in this direction but which does not mention *large fish*, but I am sure it is implied:

Upon a river bank serene
A fisher sat where all was green
 And looked it

He saw when light was growing dim
A fish, or else the fish saw him
 And hooked it

He took with high erected comb,
The fish, or else the story, home,
 And cooked it

Recording angels by his bed
Heard all that he had done or said,
 and booked it

The words 'patience' and 'hopeful' are ones often used to describe the fisherman's attributes. 'I could never make a fisherman, I haven't the patience.' Arthur Ransome felt that there was nothing more trying to the patience of fishermen than the remark so often made by the profane: 'I have not patience enough for fishing.'

'It is not,' he said, 'so much the remark itself (showing a complete and forgivable ignorance of angling as it does) that is annoying as the manner in which it is said, the kindly condescending manner in which Ulysses might tell Penelope that he had not the patience for needlework.' Some people consider that 'hope' is the operative word and have been known to refer to a shoal of fishermen, if that is the correct collective noun, as 'The Band of Hope'.

There are those who have a less kind image of anglers to the point of considering them barmy or mental. If a fisherman is fortunate enough to bring home some fish there may be a number of snide remarks such as: 'Which fishmonger did you buy that from on the way home?' This must be a longstanding quip to merit it on a postcard as long ago as 1905. In

15. A 1909 version of the 'expert and novice' – quite a number of anglers must have experienced this type of situation.

Fishing, My Life's Hobby Norman McCaskie considered that there was a certain ridicule attached to the unsuccessful angler, and there is implanted in us a troubling desire not to return home with a despicable show of fish to compare with the triumphant spoils of others.

The angler is usually philosophic though about his lack of success or the success of others. This even extends to his juniors who, it would seem, are frequently more successful than their elders when it comes to fishing – the rod does not make the fisherman. Even so, anglers are competitive animals, at least judging by the number and frequency of fishing matches and competitions in which some of them indulge. However, Norman McCaskie felt that a competitive angler could hardly contemplate and recreate if he was haunted by the thought that a moment's distraction may lead to his defeat by an alert and dangerous adversary. Zane Grey, too, remarked in his book *Tales of Fishes* that he did not fish for clubs or records but for the fun, the excitement, the thrill of the game, and would rather let his fish go than not.

The philosophic resignation to frequent unrewarding days in terms of lack of fish or poor fishing conditions is aptly summed up in the poem *Fishin'*, in which one verse reads:

> There's days it's ower sunny, there's days it's ower dark
> There's days it's ower rainy, I'm wet to the sark
> There's days when it's thunder, the fish winna steer
> There's days I'm sair trachled when I'm fishin' here
> The fish winna move, the fish winna steer,
> There's aye something wrang when I'm fishin' here.

16. Another 'expert and novice' scene entitled 'Art v Motherwit'. The artist is Boëtius.

"HAVING FINE SPORT HERE."

17. The 'routine' (?) visit to the fish-monger after the day's fishing. The sender of this card in 1906 has the following comments to make: 'too windy and cold to go fishing, but we are enjoying ourselves other ways. No flirting allowed (Eh. What).'

John Buchan in *Great Hours in Sport* described fishing most admirably:

The charm of fishing is that it is the pursuit of what is elusive but attainable, a perpetual series of occasions for hope. Any hour may bring to the most humble practitioner the capture of the monster of his dreams. But with hope goes regret, and the more ardent the expectations of the fisherman the bitterer will be his sense of loss when achievement fails him by the breadth of the finest hair. It is a bitterness which is commonly soon forgotten, for the same chance may occur tomorrow or next week.

To some anglers 'hope' is transformed into a dream; a dream of an orgy of catching big fish, or hooking a fish too large to land. Such a dream is manifest in an early postcard (opposite) which depicts a number of anglers in punts, and out of them, really living it up among several fishy leviathans. Here the desire for 'excitement' is clearly shown – 'I had an exciting time' and 'Can a photo lie?' The sender's message on the back of this card simply said – 'See how others do it.'

Roderick Haig-Brown, one of Canada's finest and most humane anglers, said that going fishing meant different things to different people. There is not one way of going fishing, but many, and each has special appeal and meaning for its devotees. This was particularly true for Zane Grey, one of America's big game fish anglers early this century:

One of the truths of evolution is that not to practise strife, not to use violence, not to fish or hunt – that is to say, not to fight – is to retrograde as a natural man. Spiritual and intellectual growth is attained at the expense of the physical.

Always when I am fishing I feel that the fish are incidental, and that the reward of effort and endurance, the incalculable and intangible

I Had an Exciting Time

CAN A PHOTO LIE?

Copyright Design Registered.

18. Some fishing outing in 1911! *Can* a photo lie? Name of locality is being withheld.

19. The old image of the angler's mentality. 'Copped owt' tends to be a Yorkshire expression so maybe the asylum is Menston near Otley.

SCENE OUTSIDE ASYLUM.

Luny—What are you doing there, guvnor?
Gent—Fishing, to be sure,
Luny—Copped owt yet?
Gent—No;
Luny—COME IN HERE!

496

knowledge emanate from the swelling and infinite sea or from the shaded and murmuring stream. Thus I assuage my conscience and justify the fun, the joy, the excitement, and the violence.

The excitement and relaxation afforded by fishing must be a good tonic because fishermen are renowned for their ability to 'take a joke' and laugh at themselves, whatever the weather conditions prevailing at the time. Their humour is so unbounding that it deserves a chapter to itself.

A QUIET POOL

20. A peaceful trout stream. An air of tranquillity pervades the scene.

The Angler And His Environment

We have seen that one of the reasons people go fishing is to get away from the humdrum of everyday life. As most of us live in an urban environment that means getting out into the country, inhaling fresh, unpolluted air and enjoying the sights and sounds of the countryside. Not every angler can get into the country to fish; some may not wish to and may find it equally satisfying to sit on a canal towpath or a river bank in the heart of or close to a built-up area. As long as there are fish the anglers are perfectly happy to sit there and enjoy themselves. Good luck to them and how nice it is to be so easily satisfied. Generally speaking though, in order to fish one needs to get into the country or to the seaside. It becomes part of the pleasure of fishing. There are some though who take up fishing simply to catch fish and are quite insensitive to their surroundings. I remember well a ghillie telling me about such a person.

Trout Fishing: A likely Spot.

21. Trout fishing with the long greenheart rod which was most commonly used at the turn of the century.

The angler was busily thrashing the water when a kingfisher flew past – a brilliant flash of electric blue and chestnut contrasting sharply against the sombre hues of the river bank. 'Look, sir, there's a kingfisher!', to which remark the unhappy angler replied – 'I'm here to catch fish not to watch birds.' Such a man is to be pitied. If only he had read Romilly Fedden's *Golden Days*, where in the very first paragraph of the first chapter he says:

Would they understand, or would there be some who, when they saw us going a-fishing, merely thought we went a-catching fish? It is the spirit of fishing we would here emphasise, its immeasurable charm and mystery which ever leads us to green and flower-girt pastures, on beyond the leafy woods, where wild birds sing . . . Above all, there is the indefinable thrill of things concerning open skies, unfettered solitudes, misty dawns, and during twilights, the sights and sounds and fragrance along the river bank.

Zane Grey, a writer of fishing tales as well as westerns, stated that in his experience:

. . . the greatest pleasure has been the certainty of something new to learn, to feel, to anticipate, to thrill over. An old proverb tells us that if you wish to bring back the wealth of the Indies you must go out with its equivalent. Surely the longer a man fishes the wealthier he becomes in experience, in reminiscence, in love of nature, if he goes out with the harvest of a quiet eye, free from the plague of himself.

In most true anglers there is the makings of a naturalist. The interest an angler shows in plants and animals and his surroundings comes from the deep-seated instinct of the hunter, the last-remaining relic of his ancestors, who hunted and fished for food and to whom a keen awareness

THE RIPPLING STREAM.
Casting from a rocky ledge
Down beside the water's edge.

22. The rippling stream with the angler concentrating hard. The length of rod would tend to suggest he was fishing for salmon, but at one time trout rods were very long and made of greenheart.

of the environment was essential for survival. Robert Burton in his *The Anatomy of Melancholy* also pointed out that 'if so be the angler catch no fish, yet he hath a wholesome walk to the brookside, pleasant shade by the sweet silver streams, he hath good air and sweet smells of fine fresh meadow flowers, he hears the melodious harmony of birds.' These are words which can be attributed to Juliana Berners some centuries earlier.

A good angler can 'read' the water. He knows from experience and instinct where the fish are likely to be. The trout angler can picture in his mind's eye where the quarry is lying – behind that boulder out of the strength of the current but strategically placed to collect the food conveniently swept into the eddy behind, or close to the overhanging bank in the shade of the willow ready to collect falling insects or to dart for shelter. Similarly, the coarse angler can sum up the slow and

23-25. This series of three cards illustrates the adventure of four jolly fishermen to the accompaniment of a verse by F.E. Weatherly on the back of each card. You needed to have all three before you could enjoy the full story:

Four jolly fishermen, spruce and gay,
Went out fishing on a summer's day,
Their lines were good and their rods
were long,
And they hummed a lively and jaunty
song.
Then down they sat in the morning
shine,
And baited their hooks with bait so
fine,
But though they fished with a gay
good will,
The fish swam safe in the river still.

But still they sat, those fishermen gay,
And watched their floats in a guileless
way,
Till just as their hopes, like the sun,
rose high,
A terrible barge came drifting by.
And what those fishermen then befell,
Is really more than verse can tell,
And what was the worst of that
morning's ill.
The fish swam safe in the river still.

JUST THE DAY FOR FISHING.

Wishing you a jolly Christmas.

Happiness be thine this Christmas day.

However they soon forgot their pain,
And nimbly they sat them down again,
But they had not sat for a minute or two,
When a storm came on and drenched them through.
And each one looked at his neighbour's nose,
And each one said, as home went they,
We think we have 'caught' enough today.

A punt was a commonly used platform for fishing where access to the river bank was hindered by a thick growth of reeds and rushes. The punt was moored at either end by a pole pushed into the mud of the river bed.

These cards are actually old Christmas greetings cards which were used before postcards first appeared in 1870. They are the shape of a postcard and to all intents are a postcard except that they were sent in an envelope (just like an invitation card). It is possible to date these cards because the publishers were Hildesheimer & Faulkner who were joint producers of greetings cards between 1878 and 1885, after which they started separate businesses in the postcard publishing trade.

With best wishes for a happy Christmas.

supposedly featureless water of the sluggish lowland river and decide where best to set up his gear and bait his chosen 'swim'. The sea angler, too, can read the lie of the coast and the nature of the beach and, taking note of the state of the tide and the wind direction, select a stretch of shore likely to be most productive.

Of course there are anglers, in name only, who rely on ghillies or guides to show them where to fish. Some salmon anglers come into this category, as does the holiday angler who is taken out to sea in a launch, has his hook baited and is shown where to drop his line over the side.

Probably more trout anglers are naturalists than any other type of angler. They see their quarry rising to flies on the water surface and attempt to imitate them artificially by dressing their hooks with feathers, fur and tinsel. The tying of artificial flies is an art dating back hundreds of years. There is a certain satisfaction in catching a trout on an artificial fly you have tied yourself. Izaak Walton's friend Charles Cotton, who wrote the section on trout fishing in *The Compleat Angler*, appreciated this

26. A likely pool below the weir. A good spot on a summer's day.

27. A salmon pool on the Tay near Perth. This is the Town Water available to residents and visitors at a very reasonable price. Many anglers obviously came out on their bikes in those days.

28. An angler into a fish on the Nairn. The companion sitting on a rock is waiting with the gaff.

79. A Likely Pool.

Salmon Pool on the Tay, Perth.

THE INTAKE, RIVER NAIRN.

29. Some anglers cannot get into the country to fish and are quite content fishing in an urban environment. When the river flows through a beautiful city like Salzburg there should be no complaints. The river is the Salzach and the period about 1840.

30. Fishing on Loch Leven, Kinross-shire. This was at one time the most productive brown trout water in Scotland. It is the venue for the International Angling Competition. The castle is the one in which Mary Queen of Scots was imprisoned. Postmark 1906.

when he said: 'I know a trout taken with a fly of your own making will please you better than twenty with one of mine.'

Most true anglers are aware of their surroundings, and particularly the river. Were it not so there would be few or no fish in some of our rivers, as pollution from sewage works, paper mills, tanneries and coal mines can very quickly eliminate the fish in the rivers into which these toxic and suffocating wastes are discharged. The angler is quick to detect the presence of nauseating substances in the water, as are the fish with their lives. Were there no anglers there would be no fish in many of our rivers, as there would be no body of people demanding their protection and return, and the rivers would remain unhealthy and unable to support life. The polluters would have no fears of court proceedings, prosecutions and claims for damages. Their only concern would be from the water services

31. A bite. Suppressed excitement in the small boy, who has probably been told to 'stand back or you'll scare the fish', as Dad is about to strike. Such a scene without doubt portrays the conditions under which many small boys have been introduced to fishing. A Raphael Tuck card.

32. An interesting trade card produced in the late 1930s by a local fisherman on the Great Ouse, who catered for visiting anglers and campers. At the top of the card we can see the size limits for the various fish species, below which length they must be returned to the water. Nowadays of course opractically all coarse fish are returned to the water.

that demand a certain quality of water for their consumers. Even so, that quality need not be as high as that required by the fish, as it can, and usually is, treated chemically before being piped to our houses. To illustrate what I mean by the angler's ability to detect change in the river I will quote from Cecil, Lord Harmsworth's *A Little Fishing Book*, the chapter 'The Derelict Trout Stream':

To anybody but a fisherman the stream presented an unchanged appearance. It ran, murmuring sweetly as of yore, and keeping faithfully to its appointed channel. The moorhens flirted still in and out of its reedy banks, uttering warning cries to their inexperienced broods. The great swifts swept over its surface. I marked a kingfisher, of rosy breast and sapphire wing, flashing downstream before me. But I was mistaken when

33. The beautiful Welsh Dee near Llangollen

34. A Dartmoor trout stream where an angler can be on his own all day long.

On The Okement, DARTMOOR.

35. Salmon fishing at Llandyssul.

on near inspection I found or thought I found a change in the stream itself? The water seemed to be soiled – I can think of no better word. It was less clear and the sparkle had gone out of it. And there was a grey film on the bottom weeds . . . I left the X in a spirit of dejection. I shall never go there again, or perhaps I may live to see it restored to its former freshness and clarity!

Changes are not always for the best and anglers, like many souls, indulge in nostalgia. They may have pictures of their favourite rivers and lakes as they knew them in the past and where red letter days were had or happy holidays spent. The angling literature, too, can conjure up memories of the past, but the authors of so many fishing books dwell on the fish they have caught, how they beguiled them and advice on the best

36. Angler and dog equally expectant. Dogs have often been known to jump in and bring the fish their masters have hooked to land in their jaws.

37. An early (pre-1902) postcard depicting an angler fishing the Tweed at Abbotsford, the home of Sir Walter Scott.

38. A pleasant stretch of trout water on the upper part of the river Tweed near Peebles.

methods to use. I can think of relatively few where the author has more to say than this, which is surprising after what I have said about the angler's awareness of his environment. Is it because he thinks it is something personal in which others would not be interested, or is it his inability to portray it adequately in words? John Buchan was one who could:

One such evening I remember in the high glens about the source of Tweed, where I spent the night in the solemn fastness of the hills. Leaving a sleeping-rug in the shadow of a rock behind a belt of pines, with my rod and my creel I went up a burn which loitered down a flat upland valley. The water was flooded and clear, and made a pleasant noise twining around the corner of a weather-stained rock or winding among odorous thickets of thyme. The quietness of the hills – so great that the most

ABBOTSFORD FROM THE RIVER TWEED, NEAR GALASHIELS

FISHING ON THE TWEED NEAR PEEBLES. 213258

39. A matter of scale. Enough to start any youngster fishing. The fish could be a Chinook salmon.

40. An early Canadian postcard of the Grand Trunk Railway System – 'Bass fishing on the French River, Ontario'.

41. Trout fishing in the Nipigon River, Ontario. Probably a card printed for the Canadian Pacific Railway.

42. A good-sized rainbow trout beached at Lake Rotorua. The angler is wearing chest waders which allows him to wade out into deep water.

distant sounds fell distinctly on the ear and one heard the running of faraway waters – was enlivened by the gorgeous sunset light and the activity of bird and insect. The flash of brown bees, the wavering flight of snipe, the dart of water ousels, gave liveliness to the quiet valley. The hills stood out against the saffron sky, great violet-coloured shoulders and peaks, looking remote in the evening air. The wholesome smell of the moorlands, which stirs in man's blood strongly, had a lowland luxury in it from the crushed summer flowers.

That passage from *Scholar Gypsies* conjures up many things for many anglers, but there are few who could so clearly portray the scene. One other angling writer who has this gift is Negley Farson. If I was allowed only one angling book to take with me to a remote island, on which the

Bass Fishing on the French River, Ontario.
Grand Trunk Railway System.

39

Trout Fishing in the Nipigon River, Ontario

44. Fishing in Iceland – the Ellidaar near Reykjavik.

43. Lord of all he surveys! A Japanese fisherman sitting out on a specially constructed seat in Lake Hakone.

Bible, Shakespeare and *The Compleat Angler* were awaiting my arrival, I would take his book *Going Fishing*. Open it at any page and one can read on and imagine oneself in any of the many countries in which he has fished. Two passages from the book illustrate this well:

And so the years passed.

There are a few memories which still stand out from them. One was a night when in an 11½ ton yawl we anchored in a place called Deep Harbour, Maryland. At sunset Joe and I (he was killed at Chateau Thierry) got out our shotguns and took the dinghy ashore to go after some snipe we saw feeding along the waterline. We got three, and they were the treat of the night's dinner, with the water lapping gently against

45. Fishing on the Nordura in west Iceland. The pool is the Laxfoss.

our sides, and with a full moon rising, we lazily fished for catfish. Although we were hard up for any kind of food then, we did not care whether we caught anything or not; the night was so beautiful. We were hushed by it. I was not writing in those days, except to amuse myself; but I wanted so much to put the enchantment of that night into words that it hurt. And then as we were sitting there not talking, a hound bayed far up on the hill . . . a hound baying at the moon. I shall always remember that.

Another passage, this time during his travels in Russia, recaptures not only the scene but the political conditions prevailing:

Then one sunset we came out on a high spur of mountains where the swift-flowing rivers, the Teberda and the Kuban, met to form that eventually long lazy river wandering across the Cossack steppes. Mt Elbuz, 3000 feet higher than Mt Blanc, lay behind us, its cone of snow glowing like a living flamingo in the sunset. There were one hundred and twenty miles of unbroken snow and glaciers between its two nipples and Kazbek. And as I sat on my horse my eyes were still filled with the thunder of the previous sunset, the thunder of emotions inside me, when I sat in the saddle and looked along fifty miles of unbroken snows turning all shades of rose and indigo as night came on.

Below me now lay the junction of these two rivers, the Teberda, glacial and grey, the Kuban a vivid bottle green. Where they met they ran in two parallel bands of colour until they fused in a rapid-filled gorge about two miles from where we had come out of the pine forest. I fished this gorge at

46. Trout fishing – an old enthusiast. An attractive North American trout river. The angler could be a farmer judging by the hat and the clay (?) pipe. The card is one of Valentine's 'Artotype' series.

47. Another 'Artotype' card in the Sporting Series, this time depicting salmon fishing, probably on a river in northern Quebec.

48. Fishing for brook trout (speckled trout) in eastern Canada. This card was printed before 1902 for the Canadian Grand Trunk Railway System by Valentine's.

SPORTING SERIES
SALMON FISHING. "LANDED"

47

SPORTING SERIES

"Where the speckled Trout abound."

48

sunset that night, getting seven trout. By an accident, as it was I who put them on the ashes and embers, using some of our last butter we had bought from a shepherd tribe, they were excellent. I had forgotten them and had let them get slightly crisp. And that night a Cossack, who informed me that his official status was Instructor of Communism, ate one of them, pronounced it marvellous; but said that I was a Capitalist because I used the fly.

Sometimes when I go fishing I take a book with me. There are times when there is little fish activity and a book helps to while away the time and to rest from one's exertions, particularly after some hours of wielding a cane salmon fly rod. Some say persevere and that you will not catch fish unless your flies are in the water. Perhaps, but a rest brings one back to the water refreshed and one's power of concentration improved. I was gratified to read in John Buchan's article in the *Gentleman's Magazine* of 1893, entitled 'Angling in Still Waters', that he knew of a sheriff who was a great angler. Whenever he went out on an expedition he put a Horace in

49. The angler's Eldorado – Lake Rotorua in North Island, New Zealand. A colour-tinted postcard printed in 1920. Rotorua was one of New Zealand's lakes to which, firstly, brown trout and then rainbow trout were introduced at the end of the last century. Both species grow to a good size and sport is superb.

50. The pressure on fishing space in freshwaters and along the coast has led many anglers to take to boats on the sea. Sea fishing has, of course, always been a popular branch of angling, particularly for big game fish such as tuna. Boats such as the one illustrated are used off the coast of Nova Scotia for tuna. The angler has a comfortable seat but he usually wears a harness attached to his rod to assist him in the backbreaking work of tiring such large fish.

his pocket. When he had little success he was wont to take it out and find pleasure in the impassioned lyrics, for Horace and Ovid had a true feeling for nature.

One book which does occasionally share my fishing bag, with boxes of flies and spools of nylon, is Bruce Lockhart's *My Rod, My Comfort*. He, like Farson, was a well travelled angler and was as content to admire the scene as to catch fish. The following extract, describing fishing in Jugoslavia, is a suitable one on which to close this chapter:

At night when I came back to the primitive wooden inn where I stayed, there were fresh trout, delicious new potatoes, and home-made bread and butter to be washed down with the excellent white wine. Then lighting a pipe, I would sit at the window and listen to the serenade of shepherd's pipes and ringing voices. The moon would rise, showing the outline of the mountains in sharp and steely relief, and casting a ghostly light on the dancing waters. The casement window of my bedroom overhung the river, and I would go to bed to the soft plash of rising trout.

51. Fishing in Florida. The fish could be a bass. The bait appears to be a spoon and the reel is a multiplier. Postmark is Altamonte Springs, Florida, 14 October 1915.

Fishing with Rod and Line, Florida.

Reflections of Fishermen's Luck in Carondelet Park, St. Louis, Mo.

217916

53

LANDLORD: "There is no fishing here!"
ANGLER: "I beg your pardon, my friend, but you are mistaken, there is fishing here. I'm getting plenty!"

53. Quite a number of cartoons on this theme, frequently seen in old issues of *Punch*. Postmark 1906.

54. A joke with a religious theme – No Sunday Fishing.

Minister: "Don't you know, Johnnie, that it is wrong to catch fish on the Sabbath?"
Johnnie: "Wha's catchin' fush?"

54

FISHING HUMOUR

The followers of the Gentle Art have a number of weaknesses upon which many have made merry – the angler's habit of exaggerating the size of his catch, his patience or his impatience when the fish won't bite, the conscious or unconscious ridicule he has to endure from onlookers when he is unsuccessful and the proverbial thirst which attacks the fisherman, whether or not he catches anything. However, the angler is not slow to laugh at his own peculiarities and failings and the after-dinner jokes at the winter angling-club festivities bear witness to this. If the angler was unable to rise above the remarks made by his family and friends on returning from a fruitless day's fishing he would soon give up the sport and turn to some ball game such as golf, where no one is expecting him to bring home anything, other than perhaps a bad temper.

Just Got One Today!

55. A contemporary Canadian card on the big fish theme from English River, Ontario.

As Izaak Walton declares through his character Piscator, a good angler must not only bring an inquiring, searching, observing wit: he must also bring a large measure of hope, patience and a love to the Art.

Punch has been illustrating national humour since its beginning in 1841 and angling has had its fair share of attention. The following is an early amusing portrayal of a south country trout angler from 'The Confession of a Duffer':

No pursuit is more sedentary, if one may talk of a sedentary pursuit, and none more to my taste, than trout-fishing as practised in the south of England. Given fine weather, and a good novel, nothing can be more soothing than to sit on a convenient stump, under a willow, and watch the placid kine standing in the water, while the brook murmurs on, and

56. Irish jokes are frequent!

57. A play on the term 'foul-hooked' (ie when the fish has come to be hooked in any part of its anatomy other than its mouth!).

58. Another Irish joke. Notice comments from the bridge – the usual site for onlookers with their remarks.

FROM
"PUNCH."
                    IRISH MEASURE.
Boatman telling a fishing story: "Troth, sorr, and he was a purty fish, and just when I would be afther bringin' him to the net, if the owld rod didn't go and break in three halves!"

A FOUL CATCH!

What are ye afther Patsey?
Fishin,-they'll be crowdin in onder the bridge out av the wet.

TROUT FISHING.   HOOKED BUT NOT LANDED.

A FALSE ALARM.

perhaps the kingfisher flits to and fro. Here you sit and fleet the time carelessly, till a trout rises. Then, indeed, duty demands that you shall crawl in the manner of the serpent till you come within reach of him, cast a fly, which usually makes him postpone his dinner hour. But he will not come on again, there is no need for you to change your position, and you can always fill your basket early – with irises and marsh marigolds.

The salmon angler, too, does not escape description:

Real difficulties and sufferings begin when you reach the Cruach-na-spielbo, which sounds like Gaelic, and will serve us as a name for the river. It is, of course, extremely probable that you pay a large rent for the right to gaze at a series of red and raging floods, or at a pale and attenuated

59. An early Raphael Tuck postcard (pre-1902) illustrating a trout fishing scene with the warning that a hooked fish is not yours until it has been landed!

60. Another early Raphael Tuck card in the same 'Connoisseur' series. This one is entitled 'A false alarm'. The angler is salmon fishing judging by the fact that his ghillie is running to his aid with a gaff.

61. A later Raphael Tuck postcard, postmarked 1911, in their series of Boating and Seaside Jokes from *Punch*.

62

63

A TRIUMPHANT RETURN!

H·C·EARNSHAW

64

WHAT THE FISHERMAN
WAS GOING TO CATCH
AND — WHAT HE CAUGHT!

65

"CARRY 'EM 'OME
FOR YER GUVNOR?"

FISHING

H·C·EARNSHAW

66

62. A frequent joke on the angler's catch – old boots and kettles, etc. The artist is H.C. Earnshaw.

63. An uncomfortable and awkward place to hook oneself. There is only one solution! Not so bad when you hook yourself between the shoulders, you only need to take your coat off!

64-66. Three Earnshaw cards illustrating a skit on the angler's catch. The one depicting the angler on his triumphant return from fishing is kind, but the other two make a sly dig at his 'success'.

trickle of water, murmuring peevishly through a drought . . . Oh, how cold it is! I begin casting at the top of the stream, and step from a big boulder into a hole. Stagger, stumble, violent bob forwards, recovery, trip up, and here one is in a sitting position in the bed of the stream. However, the high india rubber breeks have kept the water out, except about a pailful, which gradually illustrates the equilibrium of fluids in the soles of one's stockings. However, I am on my feet again, and walking more gingerly, though to the spectator my movements suggest partial intoxication. That is because the bed of the stream is full of boulders, which one cannot see, owing to the darkness of the water. There was a fish rose near the opposite side. My heart is in my mouth. I wade in as far as I can, and make a tremendous swipe with the rod. A frantic tug behind, crash, there goes the top of the rod. I am caught up in the root of a pine tree high up on the bank at my back . . . I waddle out, climb the bank, extricate the fly, get out a spare top, and to work again more cautiously. Something wrong, the hook has caught in my coat, between my shoulders.

67-69. Three early American humorous cards on the big fish theme. 'They're biting well here' is a commonly used caption – pity they used the sea-living mackerel for a river scene in the last of them; the large pike, however, makes a good subject for the second scene.

It Takes Real Fishermen to Land These

86-6

70. Some old tackle shops, like chemists and fishmongers, had the symbol of their trade suspended outside their premises. Obvious bait for a midnight reveller.

They're Biting Well Here

FISHING TACKLE. E

FLIES. RODS. BAIT A'

FISHING TACKLE MAKER (DISTURBED BY FURIOUS KNOCKING AT NIGHT):—
"WHAT DO YOU MEAN BY KICKING UP THAT ROW AT THIS UNEARTHLY HOUR"

MIDNIGHT REVELLER:— "IT'SH ALL RIGHT OLE CHAPPIE, THOUGHTSH I'D TELL YOU, YOU'VE GOT A BITE"

THE WAY WE CATCH THEM HERE.

AT PORT HOPE, ONT.

"A Minnow"

71

71. A 1930 American card from Livermore Falls, Maine. The sender's message reads: 'You had better hurry home Altie Wyman seems to think there are lots of fish in these little brooks like this if his wife would let him go fishing every day.'

72. A vintage Canadian card and a vintage Canadian car. Large Walleye (?) are being beaten to death at Port Hope, Ontario.

73. The uncertainty of angling – this Bavarian angler's weight has broken the rotten bridge. Note barrel which is the traditional receptacle for holding fish alive and in which they can be taken back to the hotel.

74. The element of surprise – a freshwater crayfish forming an attachment for his captor. Note leather knee boots of companion.

73

74

Scene Near MOULTONBORO, N. H.

75

Yes, we have all experienced such discomforts but we are able to look back and laugh at the many situations with which we are faced, probably more than any other outdoor sportsman experiences.

Mr Punch is not the only author to laugh at the angler although, as he says, he presents them so jovially that nobody laughs at them more heartily than his victims. In 1887 F.C. Burnand edited an amusing text, based on Izaak Walton's work, entitled *The Incompleat Angler*. The illustrations by Harry Furniss guaranteed its success. Izaak Walton is portrayed as a Mr Punch-like character who thoroughly enjoys encounters with milkmaids between giving lessons on angling to the Hunter (Venator):

Piscator   But see! There in the meadow are two simple milkmaids tending the sheep. We will speak them so fairly that they shall be glad to give us a leg of young lamb in exchange for our pike.
Venator   O, Master, the more buxom of the pair would be a fit helpmate for an angler.
Piscator   Why so?
Venator   She is so *Chubby*!

One of the most renowned and well-loved anglers of the earlier part of this century was H.T. Sheringham. He had a great sense of humour and could see the funny side of the sport in a way from which we could all profitably benefit. His *Fishing: Its Cause, Treatment and Cure* is full of amusing incidents. This, from the chapter 'Voces Populi':

An angler is plying his art in mid-stream below a bridge which carries the London road across a stream not many miles from town. On the bridge are spectators who lean with their elbows on the parapet, occasionally spit into the water, and from time to time comment on the proceedings. Now and then a char-a-banc rumbles across the bridge, the voices of its occupants generally contributing something to the discussion. The angler, who has suffered these things before, is able to make a fair pretence of deafness.

75-78. Scenes near Moultonboro, New Hampshire. Probably a popular fishing resort where the demand for this type of card was assured.

Scene Near MOULTONBORO, N. H.

Scene Near MOULTONBORO, N. H.

78

Le dégouté.

79

80

Female voice   Wot's that man doing in the water?

1st Male Voice   Fishing, M'ria. That's wot e's doin'.

Female Voice (disappointed)   Oh, fishing! Thought 'e was lookin' for corpses or something o' that. People as 'ad drownded themselves.

Squeaky Voice   Come on, 'Enery, 'ere's a man in the water.

2nd Squeaky Voice   Look at 'is rod. Ain't it a long 'un? I'd like to have a rod like that.

1st Squeaky Voice   Wot's 'e fishin' for?

2nd Squeaky Voice   Jacks, 'e is. Tommy Simmins, 'e 'ad a jack yesterday. Nine inches long it was.

1st Squeaky Voice (excited)   I can see 'is 'ook. Ain't it a little 'un? All over feathers. Ain't he got no worm or anything? Hi, mister, you ain't got no bait on your 'ook. It's all over feathers!

Many Voices (from char-a-banc)   What ho, tiddlers! Felix kept on walking?

79. Very French! An obvious solution for those who don't like handling earthworms.

80. A trade postcard produced by Guinness. Very much a 'My Goodness, my Guinness' theme.

81. A Loch Ness version of *Thursday* – see Plate 7. The monster is often sighted in the vicinity of the Fort Augustus monastery.

Many of you will have experienced that situation. I have, some time in the past, but I don't think it happens much nowadays. Maybe people don't lean over bridges so much.

As well as people making fun of anglers, anglers, too, sometimes ridicule each other or play practical jokes. The earliest angler to do this was probably Cleopatra:

> *Charmian*   'Twas merry when
> You wager'd on your angling; when your diver
> Did hang a salt-fish on his hook, which he
> With fervency drew up.
>
> *Cleopatra*   That time – O times!
>
>   (*Antony and Cleopatra*, Act 11, scene V)

We don't always react to a joke in the manner it is meant to be taken and the *Angler's Mail* for 16 November 1977 refers to roused emotions at an angling match under the headline 'Punch follows taunt in big-match

82. Another early American card on the large fish theme. This one, entitled 'Sights on our travels through Wakefield, Mass.' has a message on the back which reads: 'This is an American spratt. Can they catch any in Poole [Dorset] like this?'

Sights on our Travels through Wakefield, Mass.

Published by A. H. Thayer

Copyright by The Frank W. Swallow Post Card Co., Inc.

83. Trout fishing at Great Lake, Tasmania. Another card on the large fish theme. This reservoir, sixty miles from Hobart, is noted for its large trout. The card was sent in 1949 and since that time other large reservoirs have been formed in Tasmania and have produced very big trout. More recently a proposed reservoir scheme was vetoed through the action of conservationists. The sender of the card remarks: 'They have a saying in Sydney "Home on the pig's back". This looks better, what do you say?'

One Of The Finest

84. Another 'joke' card to send home to show how big the fish are in these parts. The title of the card on the reverse side states: 'Bringing out a big rainbow trout. This is one of the finest ever caught in these parts.'

"CHEER UP, OLD SPORT! THAT'S NOTHING TO THE MARRIAGE KNOT!"

85

86

These Whoppers Snap at Anything

rumpus': 'Two officials were involved in an amazing punch-up on the banks of the Tyne before last week's Gurkha Open after one allegedly called the other – "a silly little man"!' An exceptional incident which, when related to other anglers, usually results in spontaneous amusement.

We have laughed at ourselves as anglers for centuries and hopefully we shall continue to do so for years to come in spite of hunt saboteurs and the like. No one has helped us to see the amusing side of our sport in recent years more than Norman Thelwell with his true-to-life angling cartoons collected together by Eyre Methuen (1967) in *Thelwell's Compleat Tangler – Being a Pictorial Discourse of Anglers and Angling*.

For those who may feel that we are the biggest laughing stock in the world let me reassure them that we are not. In two books of collected after-dinner stories related by eminent people (*Pass the Port* and *Pass the Port Again, Brann*), golfing stories outnumber fishing stories 23 to 5. Scottish stories take the lead with 66 followed by Irish and naval stories. Even clerical and judicial stories are more numerous than those on fishing. But who cares?

87. A freshwater Jaws no doubt. The sender remarks: 'I have yet to meet someone here [Manhattan] who does not either fish or shoot.'

85. Some consolation for an angler who has got his line in a fankle! This is one of Valentine's 'Bonzo' cards. The dog Bonzo was placed in many amusing situations and angling gave the artist, G.E. Studdy, plenty of scope. Studdy was familiar with angling and illustrated and was joint author with H.T. Sheringham of *Fishing: Its Cause, Treatment and Cure*.

86. The 'old and the new' in Iceland. The American (?) angler for all his modern gear – fishing waistcoat, rubber waders, etc – looks far from happy.

Thames Valley - A fair Angler

THE FAIR SEX

The Travis Commission, set up in the late 1970s to make a broad enquiry into the place occupied by angling in the British way of life, considered that angling has a masculine image that may repel, rather than attract females. It could be of course that women receive no encouragement to take up angling. In a national angling survey in 1973 a researcher stated that: 'It seems one of the attractions of angling to males is the sport's capacity to release them from domestic ties.' In other words, 'to get away from the wife for a while'. But is this really true? If it is, has it always been so? A lot of evidence from old postcards suggests that it has not and indeed it would seem that the fair sex fairly revelled in the Gentle Art at one time. It would also appear from this evidence that there are four stages in the angler's attitude to women as either true anglers or as sharers in their men's enjoyment of the sport.

The first stage is the romantic image where the angler optimistically dreams of meeting his future wife by the waterside. She may either be conveniently passing and stopping to admire the vigorous male plying his art, or she may be actually fishing herself. How nice to come upon a fair angler in distress – a hook in her skirt, her cast in an overhead branch, or playing a large fish which requires landing – the knight errant comes to the rescue and more than the fish is hooked. This is beautifully portrayed in verse in a poem from *Punch* (*Mr. Punch with Rod and Gun*, The Punch Library of Humour):

89. A lakeside or seaside version that our grandfathers in their young days might have longed to see during their fishing exploits. She would probably look better in a bikini, but this type of costume must have been all the rage at one time.

88. A fair angler by the Thames. What a vision to meet while fishing. Seems to need a hand to thread the line through the rod rings. Charming.

What are you fishing for
my pretty maid?"
"For a nice young man
kind sir," she said.
"You can fish early –
you can fish late,
But you'll never catch one
if you sit on your bait!"

90

A SPORTIVE SONG

(A sojourner in North Britain goes
salmon-fishing with a new young woman)

1.

Far from the busy haunts of men,
Mid hazel, heather, gorse,
You are the Beauty of the glen,
And I the Beast, of course,
I fetch and carry at your wish,
I wait your beck and nod,
And yet your soul is with that fish,
Your ardour in your rod.

2.

You utter not a word; your wrist
Must surely be of steel;
For, let your captive turn or twist,
You never spend the reel,
But with your eye fast fixed you stand –
Diana with a hook –
Determined that good grilse to land,
And bring your fly to book.

3.

Well done! He weakens! With the gaff
I'm ready for the prey.
And now you give a little laugh
That means 'He must give way!'
'Look out!' you cry. I do look out,
And then I lose my head.
You've missed the fish without a doubt,
But captured me instead!

91. Leap year figures in this card, with a woman angler successfully baiting her hook with a sizeable bag of money. She seems to have a creelful of 'gents' already! The artist is the well-known early picture postcard artist, Lance Thackeray.

92. A few well-dressed men soon to be 'hooked'. Obviously it's her money they are after – or is she fishing for young men?

93. How 'dishy' can you get? From the series Sporting Girls. The artist, Dudley Hardy, specialised in glamour.

90. An early example of a so-called 'comic' or risqué card. The sender, a lady called Flancy, has written at the bottom of the verse 'its all right, darling' and, on the reverse side of the card, 'look at me blushing'. The drawing is by the 'comic' artist Donald McGill who, as early as 1904, was the major exponent of the doubtfully captioned seaside card. Post-mark 1909.

92   93

94

FISHING

S. HILUESHEIMER & Co LTD LONDON & MANCHESTER.

Copyright.   FISHER MAIDENS.   Laura Le Roux.

I'm told — there was a great Swell on the water on Wednesday. N'est-ce pas.

94. Another nice 'popsie' – seems to like fishing in the winter moonlight, as good a time as any I suppose for, according to Izaak Walton, it's the best time for perch. She requires some assistance as she has put her reel on to the rod upside down – not surprising in the dark! This card, published by Philco, was posted in 1905. The earliest known year of posting of a Philco card is 1904.

95. The Fisher Maidens. Obviously the first stage or the romantic image. As a postcard printed prior to 1901 the message has to be written on the picture side of the card; the reverse side is for the address only. I wonder who the 'great swell' was. The clue for the receiver is written in the margin – 'with Enie. Think.'

SHE FORMED AN ATTACHMENT FOR ME.

96

97

98

The second stage is now reached and our fair angler accompanies her man either as a spectator giving gentle advice, as a silent admirer, or for gentle flirtation during idle moments – and almost certainly the provider of a picnic lunch.

For our third stage we assume our couples have married. Now, if the young wife was not already an angler, it is not enough for her simply to sit and admire. She must share her husband's pleasure. Suitable attire and equipment is purchased and she allows her husband to show her how it is done, for a while at any rate. She has every intention of quickly showing him how to catch more, and bigger, fish. This stage is usually the last with most males. Children arrive and the fair angler voluntarily withdraws from the scene. She may return to the sport when the children are older or have grown up and left home, or she may be relegated to the book-and-knitting-brigade, members of which loyally accompany their

96. Still the first stage – the romantic Miss Jean Aylwin has caught quite a nice grilse. Postmark 1907.

97. A 'fly' caster – the future husband well and truly hooked! The artist, Ellam, seemed to delight in this theme (see Plate 92). The message on this 1906 card reads: 'Upon my word, I expected you would have hooked something by this – I am not able to catch anything here. Expect to see your sweet face soon.'

98. Fishing for Jack – the lovely lady is after Jack while her intended is fishing for Jack (young) pike, not eels as the sender assures us. It makes a nice picture and is printed pre-1901.

husbands as far as the waterside. This is the fourth stage and one associated with more mature or senior years.

Over the years there have been a number of very famous women anglers. Pride of place goes to Miss Georgina Ballantine who caught the heaviest salmon ever taken on rod and line in Great Britain. This was a 64 lb salmon taken from the River Tay in 1922. Queen Elizabeth the Queen Mother is another excellent salmon angler who no doubt had a great influence on her grandson, the Prince of Wales, who is now a most competent salmon angler. Probably one of the most impressive of women anglers, noted for her salmon fishing achievements and superhuman endurance, was the late Mrs Jessie Tyser of Gordonbush Estate in Sutherland. Her river was the Brora and the number of days on which her catches of salmon reached double figures are innumerable: on quite a

99. Another, more sophisticated, woman fishing for Jack. She could have just dismounted from her horse. The inset picture proves she was successful. A Lance Thackeray/Raphael Tuck collaboration. Postmark 1907.

100. A summer's day at the end of a pier is a most promising place to attract an admirer. Could be on his knees to propose but most likely just to put bait on the hook.

101. More suitably attired for the occasion than our lady on the pier, but most elegant.

THE GENTLE ART OF FISHING

After Jack.

L Thackeray

Up Stream.

102. Not all affairs are without difficulties. Here an elderly maiden aunt acts as chaperone to prevent any unseemly behaviour. Postmark 1913.

103. Woman's sensible advice is not always valued, but her company can soothe frayed nerves. Very much stage two, but to give advice rather than admire.

number of days her catch soared into the twenties. She brought up her sons well and they are now both excellent anglers, particularly Richard.

The history of women anglers goes a long way back in time and their role in this sport can be traced from the angling literature to which they modestly contributed. They made their mark right from the start and one of the earliest fishing books – *The Treatise of Fishing with an Angle*, first printed in 1495 in the second *Book of St Albans* – was attributed to Dame Juliana Berners, who, according to legend, was a nun and a sportswoman. The earliest manuscript of *The Treatise* dates back to 1450, almost two hundred years before *The Compleat Angler* was published. Juliana Berners was not the first woman angler though. This position would seem to go to Cleopatra, at least according to Shakespeare:

> *Cleopatra*   Give me mine angle; we'll to the river: there –
> My music playing far off I will betray
> Tawny-finn'd fishes; my bended hook shall pierce
> Their slimy jaw; and, as I draw them up,
> I'll think them every one an Antony,
> And say, 'Ah, ha!' you're caught.
>
> (*Antony and Cleopatra*, Act 11, scene V)

In 1683 the third edition of *The Accomplished Lady's Delight* was published with a twenty-page section on angling. This book, too, was attributed to a woman, a Mrs Hannah Wolley. Then, almost two hundred years later, Diane Chasseresse, the pseudonym for Mrs Walter Crayke, produced *Sporting Sketches* which contained four chapters on salmon and trout fishing. A major work by a bevy of women anglers came out in 1892. This was *The Gentlewoman's Book of Sport* edited by Lady Greville. There were five lady contributors covering many aspects of fishing. Lady Colin Campbell wrote a chapter on trout fishing, as did

"THEY WOULD HAVE BEEN NIBBLING—
BUT *for you*"

"YOU CAN'T CATCH FISH BY
SWEARING AT THEM."

Cobham.

106. Stage three, where the wife shares her husband's pleasure of fishing. There's something wrong here as the wife has taken over – the husband and dogs are relegated to the watching role. Both have come by bicycle.

Miss Starkey; Mrs Steuart Menzies and Diane Chasseresse contributed chapters on salmon fishing, and the latter also produced one on catching saithe or coal fish; finally, the fifth authoress, Mrs Stagg, wrote on bass and tarpon fishing.

Relatively few other books dealing with angling have been written by women since then. Mrs Hilda Murray had *Echoes of Sport* published in 1910 which had two chapters on fishing and Mrs Victor Hunt wrote *Hunting, Shooting and Fishing* in 1953. In 1980 Patricia King had the fishing diaries of her aunt, Muriel Foster, published. Muriel Foster was not only a sensitive woman angler but she was also an accomplished artist and the sketches which illustrate her diaries make it undoubtedly one of the most charming of fishing records ever to have been kept. On the other side of the Atlantic, where the women are said to wear the pants,

104. A husband and wife team. This little lady is 'doing herself proud' and has a nice bass on the end of her line. The card is postmarked Bristol, Connecticut, 1908. It is a trade card of the Horton Manufacturing Co advertising 'Bristol' steel fishing rods which, as the advert states on the reverse side, 'Always give satisfaction. Beware of cheap imitations. Look for our trade mark.' The artist is Oliver Kemp.

105. Very swish – looks as though she can cast a good line. Hat most suitable for hooking flies into and also for wrapping the odd cast around the hat band.

107. A close study of the people in the boat will reveal that the person fishing is a woman. Her husband or gentleman friend has been left to wade out and fish down the pool after her.

The Deveron, Duff House Water

American women anglers have also put pen to paper. Mrs Oliver C. Grinnell, and others, produced *American Big Game Fishing*, published by the Derrydale Press in 1935. Chris Farrington in 1951 showed that women could fish in her book *Women Can Fish*, while Beatrice Cook wrote a fishing widow's saga in 1944 entitled *Till Fish Us Do Part* and in 1955 followed it with a sequel with an equally enigmatic title, *Truth is Stronger than Fishin'*.

Now, with emancipation, the women seem to have made their point and no longer have the time to write about such trivial matters. Are there fewer serious women anglers now? It is difficult to know which country nowadays has the most women anglers per head of the population but it is probably Iceland, a country which, until after the Second World War, produced few anglers of either sex.

"DON'T FISH WITH YOUR BAIT TOO NEAR THE BOTTOM, DEAR!"

108. Familiarity breeds contempt, definitely the end of stage three, no romance here and certainly no angling skill. One of the Bamforth comic cards so often seen in shops at seaside resorts.

109. The fair sex very much in charge at stage three. 'Jack is an enthusiastic fisherman, but he says the next time he goes fishing with a woman – But why repeat such language?' The card is published by James Henderson & Sons who were in production in 1904 with their Pictorial Comedy series by C. Dana Gibson. This particular card is postmarked 1910 from Colintraive, Argyllshire.

109

110. A husband and wife team well set up for the sport.

Well hooked.

We should not finish this chapter without letting the women, anglers or not, have the last word. The milk-woman and her daughter in Burnand's *The Incompleat Angler* (after Master Izaak Walton) have this to say: 'We both love anglers, they be such honest, civil, quiet men.' A feeling shared, no doubt, by many good wives! Perhaps all of us anglers have experienced a similar dialogue to the one described in the *Art of Angling* (1577) on the angler's return from his sport:

Piscator How now, wife, is the broth ready?
Wife Indeed, I have had good leisure, Good, Lord Husband. Where have you been all this day? Have you dined?
Piscator No, truly. My first bread is yet to eat since you saw me, therefore let my supper be ready as soon as maybe.
Wife So will I, but what have you brought?
Piscator Fetch me a platter and you shall see.
Wife Here is one. Shall I take them out?
Piscator No dame, I will take them out and lay every sort by themselves. How say you, wife, is there not a good dish?
Wife I am glad now that I did not throw an old shoe after you this morning.

111. A long skirt does not deter this young woman in her pursuit over the boulders after a runaway salmon. The gillie rushes to her assistance well armed with gaff and net to land the prize. The appropriate refreshment for the celebration protrudes from his left-hand pocket. The artist is Lawson Wood who was a freelance contributor to illustrated magazines and was an active worker for animal welfare. Date of postmark is 1906. The publisher is Misch & Stock's and the card is one in the 'Anglers' series.

A HIGHLAND FISHERMAN.

CHANGING FASHIONS

As in all field sports, fashions change over the years both in the type of garments worn and the material with which equipment is made. In no part of angling has this been more apparent than in the type of material used for rod-making. Juliana Berners refers to hazel, willow and aspen being the most suitable trees from which to take a 'fair, smooth staff' which must be cut between Michaelmas and Candlemas. Later, rods were made from other woods – hickory, lancewood, greenheart, ash and fir. Sometimes two or three of these woods were used in the same rod – the butt or lower joint being made from either hickory, ash or fir and the top joint of either greenheart or lancewood. Often coarse fishing rods were made of unspecified wood (sometimes rosewood) with a lancewood top joint. Another combination was mottled cane with a lancewood top. Another type of cane used was Spanish reed cane. These materials were still being used by some tackle manufacturers for rod-building in the 1940s and early 1950s.

Most salmon rods at one time were made of either washaba (bow wood), hickory or greenheart. James Younger, the St Boswell's shoemaker, gives a good description of making a salmon rod with red hickory. Greenheart though was most probably the most popular material for fly rods for both salmon and trout and this wood remained a favourite for many years and many anglers preferred it to bamboo which later came to be used for most fly rods and spinning rods. Greenheart, imported from British Guiana and used for harbour piling because it was resistant to the attacks of the teredo wood borer, has a soft, supple action for fly-fishing and a good spliced greenheart rod was a treat to use. The Grant vibration spliced greenheart salmon fly rod was probably the best rod on the market in the early part of this century and was in use well into the 1950s. Unfortunately greenheart becomes brittle and snaps without warning. I lost two top joints in this way while playing salmon on two consecutive days. I landed one with the top joint hanging on the cast

112. A highland fisherman. The rod is probably made of greenheart; the large reel is made of brass.

113. Two worthies, with standard caps, suits and watch-chains and panniers rakishly slung over the right shoulder. Both are smoking pipes with wind-protecting covers and both have a flower in the left lapel. It was not unusual for Englishmen to go fishing thus attired in the early part of this century. The fact that this card only required a halfpenny stamp for inland postage indicates that it was printed prior to 1918, as in that year the inland postage rate was raised to a penny.

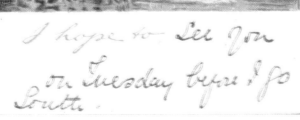

I hope to See you on Tuesday before I go South.

114

A KEEN SPORTSMAN.

A good bit of water.

116. This angler is wearing the usual garb of the Scots salmon angler in the early part of the century. The 'breeks' were of various cuts but the deerstalker was pretty standard. Waders were optional and many anglers were prepared to get their feet wet rather than be lumbered with heavy waders which make walking difficult. Probably a greenheart rod with what appears to be a metal reel.

above the salmon's head, but lost the other. For this sort of reason, greenheart gradually went out of fashion. In any case bamboo was also being used and was a much better, but more expensive rod material, particularly when rent and glued-up to become what is known as split cane.

Split-cane rods were built for all forms of fishing and were rods *par excellence* for many years. Some were given steel centres for added strength but they were not all that popular. Later split-cane rods were given extra strength by being impregnated with preservatives. The spliced, impregnated split-cane rod is still used and, while heavier than a similar length of rod made of modern materials, is preferred by many anglers. Steel rods were on the market for some years. They were made in England, Germany and the USA but were not all that popular and must have been dangerous in thunderstorms.

114. Carp fishing. The rod, because of its light colour, looks as though it is made of lancewood. A Raphael Tuck card printed prior to 1902 and postmarked 1903.

115. An Edwardian angler with a greenheart rod with what appears to be a wooden reel. The angler is wearing waterproof canvas chest waders and a pair of boots to protect the canvas feet of the waders.

117. 'Breeks' and deerstalker again, and no waders. Both anglers have large greenheart rods and the angler looking on has a very big, wide-drum wooden reel. It could be one of the old reels made by Mallochs of Perth.

Since the end of the Second World War many more materials have been available for rod-building. The first of these was glass fibre. This is a good and strong material and is used to make both hollow and solid fibre-glass rods. These are lighter and cheaper than split cane and almost indestructible – almost! They are not affected by the damp and do not warp. However, if a cow treads on them and there is a clean break that is it, while with a wooden rod one can always make a splice and, although the rod is then slightly shorter, it is almost as good as new.

Two new materials are rapidly replacing both split cane and glass fibre. One of these is carbon fibre and the other, and most recent, boron. Carbon-fibre rods were intially very expensive and prone to trouble: they were found to break even more unexpectedly than greenheart; they conduct electricity, and there has been at least one fatality through the

Safe Landed.

MARTIN AUTOMATIC FISH REEL CO., ILION, N.Y.

Mart: Almost There

119

conduction of an electric current along one of these rods; and they are rather soft and do not have the stamina or 'guts' of a split-cane rod. However, some of the early teething troubles are now remedied and most anglers who can afford their higher price are switching over to carbon fibre. They certainly throw a good line. Now boron rods are on the market and no doubt other materials will be used in the future.

The range of materials used for reels has been almost as wide as that for rods. The first reels were made of wood, later of brass, then of steel with a gun-metal finish, aluminium, bakelite and various alloys.

Lines have also evolved as more materials have become available. They were originally made of horse hair, with two, three or more hairs being twisted or plaited together depending on the thickness of the line required. Horse-hair leaders, spliced on to the end of a silk line, were still

118. Safe landed. A trout angler with a split-cane rod, easily distinguished by the frequent bindings along the rod seen clearly through a magnifying glass. The reel is probably made of aluminium. Postmark 1910.

119. Some early fishing reels in the USA were Automatic. The above is an early trade card produced by the Martin Automatic Fish Reel Co in 1906.

120. This is a most interesting postcard as it illustrates a unique method of salmon fishing on the river Shannon at Hermitage, Castleconnell, near Limerick, using the Castleconnell rod. In the swift part of the river angling is carried out by means of 'dragging'. The cot or punt is launched and poled with steel-shod poles up to the head of the current, then three rods are put out and line is released until the flies are 18 to 20 yards below the cot, which is then paddled backwards and forwards across the stream. If a fish is hooked the cot is taken into shore and the fisherman landed to finish his fight on dry land. In the picture the boatman is standing in the stern of the cot with his pole.

used well into the 1940s. They were pleasant to use, providing it was not too windy, and they made a good link between the reel line and the cast which was often made from a single horse hair.

Horse hair was replaced by flax, cord and silk. Flax lines were usually braided, while silk lines were twisted or braided and could be used either dressed, with pure oil injected with an air pump, or undressed. Floss silk lines were also used when a light but strong line was needed for dapping or blow-line fishing. Lines made from natural fibres needed to be dried after use and they required a grease floatant if they had to remain on the water surface as in dry fly fishing. How well I remember, when fishing stopped for lunch, hooking my fly to a tree or post and running the line off the reel and propping my rod up so that the line was left stretched out to dry like a clothes line. Nowadays these silk lines have been all but

Angling at Hermitage, Castleconnell, near Limerick.

replaced by thicker, plastic-coated lines, which either float, without any additional application of floatant, or sink. Sinking lines are made to sink slowly, fast or very fast. Very fast sinking lines often have a lead core which hastens the process. These are banned on some waters as they make foul-hooking fish all too easy. They have also led to electrocution when caught up on overhead power lines!

The advent of nylon made the manufacture of spinning lines extremely simple. Silk spinning lines were bothersome things which always seemed to get knotted, particularly when wet. Fly casts and leaders for coarse fishing can be made up from spools of nylon as required. The old horse-hair casts were certainly a treat to use but, like silkworm gut, which replaced horse hair, needed soaking before use. I think I would still use horse hair, or silkworm gut if they were available, for all their drawbacks.

121. Coracle fishing is chiefly associated with the Welsh Dee and Usk and some of the smaller Welsh rivers. In the main stream the paddler guides the coracle so that it avoids any just-submerged rocks, and holds it up a little as he passes through a favourite pool. If he wishes to ascend the river, he must hug the edges and go wherever the stream is weakest. The usual manner of holding it against the current is by securing it to a tree with a long rope, which is progressively paid out, or with a stone attached to a rope which functions as an anchor which can be lifted and dropped as desired. The usual length for the rod employed is 12 feet. When a salmon has been hooked it is usual for the angler to be landed so that he can play it from the bank. Occasionally he will be forced to follow it downstream. The angler in this picture is fishing the Welsh Dee near Llangollen. A close inspection of the card with a magnifying glass reveals that he is either into a fish or his line is hooked-up in a tree on the opposite bank!

122. An interesting picture of a catch of pike and bass at Bowman's Resort, Gladwin, Michigan, postmarked 1938. Of particular interest are the accessories – a live bait can on the right of picture, a black japanned tin tackle box on the left, a gaff leaning against the canoe and two rods, one with a multiplier reel which has been used for fishing with plug baits. The three plug baits are lying to the left of the reel close to the head of the large bass. The structure of the canoe is also of interest. The message reads: 'We are now in the backwoods and I mean that. Plenty of food and beer. Cold as hell at nite, have fire in stove before going to bed. Fish have been catching hell and have had plenty of luck.'

But perhaps I would not catch as many fish, as the diameter of those could never be reduced to the fineness of nylon of the same breaking strain. Then, of course, with horse hair, flies were dressed direct on to eyeless hooks to which short lengths, or droppers, of horse hair had been previously whipped. So if you wanted to change your fly you had to pull your cast apart to remove the dropper, or attach a new point if it was the tail or point fly that had to be changed.

Artificial flies have evolved over the years from simple dressings incorporating the fur and feathers of our native fauna to exotic creations dressed with the plumes and crests of ornate tropical birds. Nowhere is this better seen than in the development of the salmon fly in the last century. Initially the salmon fly was a large dowdy object but then the Victorian era marked its age of pomp and circumstance on salmon fishing. The plumage of beautiful birds came back from the Empire's distant lands to be incorporated into new and elaborate salmon fly dressings which were soon to be the subject of a treatise by Kelson and to

"The Spey, Carron Moray."

123. An angler in chest waders fishing the Spey with a greenheart rod of about 16 feet.

124. A trout angler selecting a fly from his fly book. The line seems to be very light and wavy, which makes me think it is a plaited horsehair leader which were common in those days and could still be found in the 1940s. The angler is wearing waterproof canvas thigh waders. A pre-1902 card, post-marked April 1903.

"Selecting the Fly."

161 York Street
April 3/03. "A nice spot this
The Wrench Series, No. 1569
No place for you. Mab.
letter
followme

125-127. Well dressed salmon flies, from paintings by Christine Kirk, ARCA.

become the manual of every fly dresser. Nowadays these lovely and imaginative creations – with names like Elizabeth of Glamis, Lady Caroline, Green Highlander, Jock Scott, Silver Doctor, and Thunder and Lightning – have been replaced by hair-winged flies. Part of the reason for this is undoubtedly the cost of materials and the import restrictions on some birds' plumage, but there is no doubt that the hair-wing flies give a more life-like action to the fly.

Since the days of 200 AD, when the Macedonians were hauling trout from the River Atraeus using artificial flies, trout anglers have endeavoured to lure their quarry with imitations of aquatic insects. These imitations, or dressings, are numbered in their thousands. The earlier dressings were crude by later standards and were usually employed beneath the water's surface in an attempt to imitate the larval fly or nymph as it comes to the surface to hatch. Towards the end of the last century a number of trout anglers on the southern chalkstreams developed floating imitations which required more skill in their presentation to the fish, and these 'dry-fly' purists came to consider the

Disciples of Izaak Walton.

128. Disciples of Izaak Walton. Anglers out in force, probably after coarse fish. Peak caps and bowlers were the conventional headgear of the artisan angler of the time. Postmark 1908.

use of the longer-established 'wet flies' a rather chuck-and-chance-it approach to trout fishing.

The floating and imitative properties of a dry fly depend upon the quality of the main feather which is used in its dressing; this is wound round the 'neck' of the hook immediately behind the 'eye' to resemble the wings and legs of the fly. These feathers are called hackles, and come from the neck of the barnyard fowl, the rooster producing a superior feather to that of his harem. The Old English Gamecock, or fighting cock, and some of the Jungle Cocks produce the finest quality hackles both in structure and colour. The quality of the feathers used for the hackle became an obsession with fly-tiers and dry-fly trout anglers and it was not long before Game Fowls were being bred simply for their hackles.

With the advent of reservoir fishing for brown and rainbow trout, flies

129. A present-day trout angler in New Zealand fishing the Tongariro River. Rubber thigh waders now replace the old waterproof canvas stocking waders. The rod seems to be made of glass fibre.

have, in the last decade, taken on many new guises, and strange creations are now pulled through the water at varying speeds to mimic small fish and various bugs. One is bewildered by the names given these feathered lures – muddler minnows, baby dolls, Sweeney Todd, streaker, pearly nobbler, Jersey Herd, Ace of Spades and popping bug. They can hardly be called flies; at least the dry-fly purist would not consider them such.

The changes in anglers' clothing have been equally considerable and often bizarre. Waterproof availability has risen several hundred-fold since the end of the Second World War and certainly this type of clothing has become much more comfortable. The early oilskins were heavy and hot and frequently became tacky and unwearable after long use. However, it is the footgear which has probably seen the greatest changes.

In the days of Scrope in the last century there were no rubber waterproof boots. The angler had to put up with the cold water if he decided to wade unless, of course, he wore the heavy leather knee boots worn regularly by our deep sea fishermen at that time. Our forefathers were either hardier, or more foolhardy, than we today. Scrope had a rule-of-thumb concerning wading which nowadays would send us to our beds with heavy colds at the very thought:

Never go into the water deeper than the fifth button of your waistcoat [he does not say whether it is the fifth from the top or fifth from the bottom]; even this does not always agree with tender constitutions in frosty weather. As you are likely not to take a just estimate of the cold in the excitement of the sport, should you be of a delicate temperament, and be wading in the month of February when it may chance to freeze very hard, pull down your stockings and examine your legs. Should they be black, or even purple, it might be as well to get on dry land; but if they are only rubicund, you may continue to enjoy the water, if it so pleases you.

Rubber waders were not commonly used until the 1940s and most salmon and trout anglers wore waterproof canvas stocking waders of either thigh or chest size. The waders were worn with socks and heavy boots to protect the feet of the waders from the abrasive action of stones and sand. Only the wealthiest of anglers could afford a comfortable pair of Hardy's 'Altona' rubber thigh waders.

For anyone wanting to make a real study of changes in fishing gear and clothing, reference should be made to the numerous fishing tackle catalogues which have been published over the years on an annual basis by firms like Hardy's, Allcock's and Farlow's. But old postcards depict the angler in action and reveal interesting aspects which the catalogue cannot produce.

will. B. Hunt

COPYRIGHT 1903
BY THE NORTH MFG CO

THE QUARRY

The angler's quarry can be conveniently divided into three categories – *game fish*: salmon, trout, char and grayling; *coarse fish* (sometimes referred to as 'pan fish' in the USA): which includes all other species of freshwater fish, a mixed lot which include roach, chub, bream and bass, the most popular quarry of the coarse angler, as well as dace, barbel, carp, perch, pike and wels or catfish; and *sea fish*: a rich variety which never fails to keep the sea angler on his toes, as in successive bites he may haul up a wide range of types – haddock, cod, whiting, plaice, dab, mackerel, skate, ray and dogfish.

Richard Gordon amusingly describes four sorts of fishing based on these categories:

1. Coarse fishing – sitting on a small folding stool under an umbrella all winter.
2. Sea fishing – windy, muscular and emetic.
3. Salmon fishing – as expensive as keeping a mistress, but much more frustrating.
4. Trout fishing – perfection in angling.

The reason that (4) is given this description is because, unlike (1), it is performed on foot rather than on the bum and a day's fishing is a day's exercise. This is true if you trout fish in rivers or from the shore of a lake, but it is certainly not the case if you sit in a drafty boat out on a wind-swept lake. There is then no opportunity for the coarse angler's umbrella and the bum is frequently sore and wet.

The attention the various categories of quarry receive depends on their accessibility and availability. Accessibility is chiefly dependent on the angler's financial status, while availability is dependent on the abundance of the quarry. For this reason coarse fish, due to their low monetary value and abundance in areas of high population density, are the most popular and most frequently angled in areas such as the Midlands of England and

130. A nice bass hooked on fly. The artist is Will B. Hunt. This is a trade card produced in 1902 by the Horton Manufacturing Co. of Connecticut.

131. Sea angling – emphasis on the booze and a little bit of wishful thinking. This is a Shadowgraph card and needs to be held up to the light – the result of which would be to see a girl wearing a bikini, face mask and flippers!

the Low Countries. Sea fish are the next most popular because this type of fishing is free and the only limitation to availability is proximity to the coast or the ability to launch out on to the briny. Trout are popular in Scotland as they are abundant and the poor relation of the noble salmon, and the opportunity to fish for them is open to all at little cost. In many parts of England this situation does not exist as good trout waters are less common than in Scotland, thus the value put on trout fishing is at the level of poor to medium quality salmon angling in Scotland, particularly on the southern chalk streams such as the Test and the Itchen. The only exception to this is on the large reservoirs scattered throughout England and Wales where the coarse angler spends part of the year when his preferred quarry are busily engaged in their nuptials. In Austria and Bavaria trout fishing is abundant and excellent, but expensive.

BLACK BASS

132. A Black Bass just hooked, with the frog bait being disgorged. The message on the back reads: 'Hooked my big fish today but lost him. Poor luck so far. Caught only one bass and that a small one. Spooning is alright though.' Perhaps there is a hidden meaning in the last sentence! Postmark 23 July 1909.

This grading in popularity or angling preference is revealed in the findings of the *National Angling Survey, 1980*, which showed that 60 per cent of the anglers went coarse fishing, 53 per cent went sea fishing and 20 per cent went game fishing. As an addition of the percentages show, some anglers participated in more than one branch of angling. More general statistics reveal that 15 per cent of all households in England and Wales contained at least one angler in 1979; 3,380,000 people in England and Wales and 354,000 in Scotland, aged twelve and over, went fishing during 1979. This was 8 per cent of the population and 15 per cent of all men and boys aged twelve and over.

Recent figures from the US Fish and Wildlife Service reveal that panfish, such as bluegills, perch and crappies, are the most popular group with 18.9 million anglers in pursuit. The next most popular fish are the

Roach.

133

Barbel and Chub.

134

133. Two roach and a smaller dace laid out by the riverside with an angler's porcupine quill float to give an idea of scale.

134. A large barbel and two smaller chub painted on the riverbank close to their natural haunt.

135. Some good perch on the feed. A shoal of feeding perch can often be located by the sight of small fish leaping from the water.

136. A very nice 'Oilette' by Raphael Tuck of a pike chasing roach. As in Plates 133-135, 138 and 139 the artist is A. Roland Knight.

largemouth and smallmouth bass with 18.3 million enthusiasts. Coming in third place, perhaps surprisingly, is the catfish with 13.4 million supporters, followed by trout with 10.7 million anglers on their trail and lastly the northern pike and walleye in a dead heat and each with 4.5 million followers. The estimates are based on the 1980 national survey of fishing, hunting and wildlife-associated recreation. Surely these statistics should deter the hunt saboteurs from trying to have angling banned!

To return to our quarry, as Arthur Ransome says in *Rod and Line*:

There are coarse fish everywhere, except in those places where men have been allowed to save their private pockets by poisoning the public water. But there are some counties in which, when man speaks of fishing, coarse fishing is meant; counties in which roach, bream, carp and tench, perch and pike are not tolerated second cousins, the poor relations of the trout and salmon, but have things all their own way and yield precedence to none.

Coarse fish live a charmed life in the United Kingdom as, after capture, they are returned alive to their water at the end of the day's fishing. Even the minutest of specimens are welcomed by the match angler – as little as an ounce might make the difference between winning and losing an important competition. Few coarse anglers would consider eating their quarry, but a record-size fish might have to be kept to enable the experts to decide whether the fish was a pure-bred specimen or a hybrid. Several coarse fish species, particularly the carp family, have the vulgar habit of hybridising. There are, for instance, roach/bream hybrids, roach/chub hybrids and roach/rudd hybrids, all of which makes it difficult to claim a new weight record for some of these species.

Many coarse fish are noted for their carbohydrate diet, at least that is what the angler gives them. Roach are fond of bread, carp love potatoes and chub adore bread and cheese. These species do eat animal protein as well and one of their favourite sources for this is the larva of the bluebottle, variously called the maggot or gentle; in the pupal or chrysalis form it is known as a 'caster'. H.T. Sheringham gives a nice account of roach fishing by a Mr Swimms:

I was down at Backwater on Saturday for a bit of roaching. It was very windy all day, and the only swim that would fish comfortably was by the haystacks. The water was just right, but the roach were not on. I tried crust, wheat, gentles, red paste and white paste, and only got little things all morning. Then after lunch I got a bit tired of it, so I put on a bit of seed cake from my lunch and got a half-pounder at once. After that I got three

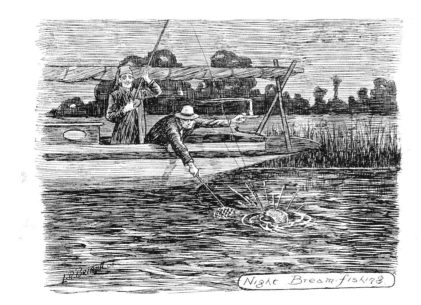

137. A leisurely form of fishing for a leisurely type of fish. Bream take a bait well during darkness. It looks as though the angler has his night-cap on!

138. Something which all trout anglers long for – a well-hooked trout fighting hard and jumping to free itself.

139. A sight for sore eyes!

more, and then the seed cake was all finished. I wish I'd had some more or eaten less.

Another popular bait is luncheon meat, particularly canned luncheon meat, and empty luncheon meat cans are unfortunately all too often left to litter the canal or river bank after big angling competitions.

One species of coarse fish which tends to be a law unto itself is the barbel. Many writers say that fishing for barbel needs a great expenditure of worms and faith. The river is enriched with a thousand lobworms daily for a week to induce the barbel to become 'hooked' on worms and then one angles for him. They feed in fast-flowing water where one needs to anchor one's line to the river bed with a lead weight. Called legering, it is a sure and quick way of losing lots of tackle.

The pike, too, requires specialist attention. It is a carnivore and eats fish, young ducks and gulls and water voles and the like. The old-fashioned way of catching pike was to fasten an array of treble hooks – referred to as a Jardine snap-tackle – to a lively roach or gudgeon and let it go for a swim close to the weed beds where the pike tend to lurk. The live bait was kept suspended in the water by a series of floats – one or two large pike floats and a small pilot float. When master pike seized the unfortunate roach or gudgeon and made off with him the large floats would disappear into the depths, in pursuit as it were. It was considered time to strike the hooks into the well-armoured jaws once the upper pilot float was also pulled below the surface. Nowadays the various spinning lures – spoons, devons and plugs – have almost replaced this method.

Trout are pursued with various lures, but the most common one is the artificial fly. The artificial comes in three forms – dry, wet and the nymph. Dry fly is considered the highest form of the art and dry-fly purists are a special breed, as we may gather from the following conversation recorded by H.T. Sheringham:

Trout—The First Leap

138

Salmon and Trout.

139

A. What do you think of that for a pale watery?

B. Not bad, not bad at all. Very nice, in fact. But there's a shade too much white in the third segment, and the right seta is about two millimetres too long.

A. Yes, you're quite right. Exactly what I said. They *will* make these silly mistakes. But for a shop fly it's not bad. Hullo what's that?

B. A rise, or was it a dabchick? No, it was a rise I think. I can't see what he's taking. *(Raises his binoculars, slung round his neck, to his eyes)* There's an olive coming down over him.

A. *(who has also brought his binoculars into action)* He wouldn't have it. Ah, I thought so. He's bulging. He was doing that yesterday. He's no good.

B. Aren't you going to have a chuck?

A. No, he isn't rising.

B. He might take a medium olive.

A. *(with a little scorn in his voice)* Oh yes, he might *take*. There was a period when I should have had that fish out with a Wickham in no time. But I don't care about that sort of thing now, naturally.

B. *(still looking regretfully at the fish which is now feeding with vigour)* Yes, perhaps you're right. But it looked that time as though he took a fly, an iron blue I believe.

A. Well, try a female iron blue over him yourself.

B. No, no, my dear fellow, he's your fish. I'm off downstream. There's a good trout at the third stile I want to interview, and the rise seems to be beginning. Well, goodbye.

A. Goodbye.

(B Takes his rod, goes off downstream and is soon out of sight.
A gets up from the seat, goes to his rod, ties a large Wickham to the end of the cast and proceeds to cover, rise, hook and land the trout, which he taps on the head, weighs and places in his creel.)

The quarry in the above encounter would have been a brown trout. Since that time the American rainbow trout has increased its range in European rivers and lakes as the result of widespread introductions from trout farms. This dandefied fish is a respectable enough fellow in his native waters of western North America, but when reared in stewponds he assumes a rather moth-eaten, fin-bitten appearance and, owing to his unseasonable habit of spawning in the spring, is at his slimiest worst when our native brown trout is gaining in condition after a winter's post-nuptial fast. However, rainbows grow fast and make a fuss when hooked, which is considered sporting.

Our ancestors would be quite surprised if they were to return to some of their favourite haunts to fish as they would find that some of the waters were frequented by additional species. Not only has the rainbow trout appeared in many waters in the last decade or so, but the grayling is more widespread. The latter species has been introduced to several large river systems this century, including the Tweed and the Clyde. Tom Stoddart and Christopher North would have been shocked to find a grayling on the end of their line when fishing their beloved Tweed. Other fish, too, have been moved to rivers in which they were not previously found and the barbel is a fairly recent newcomer to the Severn. The most controversial introduction was that of the zander, a species normally found in waters on the European continent. This predatory fish, which tends to hunt in packs, was put in the Great Ouse Relief Channel in East Anglia in 1963, since when it has spread and become a veritable nuisance.

The salmon is considered by many to be the ultimate quarry which it is every angler's desire to catch. Not everyone feels that way though and many trout anglers, like Christopher North, declare that:

Trout fishing is not only a more delightful amusement, but a higher art. A really good trout fisher – that is, not a trout fisher who can take trout

Six 'Aquarettes' in Tuck's 'British Freshwater Fish' series, painted by R. J. Wealthy. The reverse of the cards read – errors and all! – as follows:

140. *The Common Trout* is found in most parts of the British Isles, and reaches a length of 28 ins. It goes to the sea every year if it can. *The Vendace* is found in Derwentwater and Bassenthwaite, in the English Lake District, but is better known as a native of Castle Loch and Mill Loch at Lochmaben, in Dumfries. In length it is about 9 ins. *The Salmon* is 'anadromous', i.e. it lives both in the sea and in fresh water. It has been known to reach a weight of 70 lbs.

141. *The Grayling* is generally gregarious, and is confined to clear-running streams with pools and shallows. It reaches a length of 18 ins. *The Windermere Char* is palatable as it is beautiful, and is much valued as a dainty, both when fresh and potted. This fish thrives only in clear water, and frequents the deeper parts of the lake.

142. *The Pike* is common in the British Isles, where it is generally to be found in slow-running weedy rivers and lakes. In size it often exceeds 3 ft. It is a very ferocious and audacious fish. *The Gudgeon* is gregarious in its habits and prefers running water with a sandy or gravelly bed. It reaches in length 8 ins and more. *The Chub* frequents deep holes in clear waters, coming to the surface in warm weather. It occasionally attains a weight of between 6 and 7 lb, but this is rare.

143. *The Dace* is gregarious, and to be found in clear sharp-running streams, attaining a length of 12 ins. *The Roach* is found in shoals in clear, deep, still, or slow-running waters, gathering in very large numbers at certain spots for breeding purposes. It attains a length of 15 ins. *The Common Bream* is also gregarious, preferring quiet waters. Sixteen ins may be taken as a fair average of its size, but one has been caught 26 ins long.

144. *The Ruffe or Pope* is usually 3 or 4 ins in length, sometimes reaching 7 ins or more. It lives in shoals in deepish water in cool, shady places. *The Perch* is one of the handsomest of British freshwater fishes. It prefers ponds, or rivers where the current is slow. *The Barbel* lives at the bottom of gently flowing rivers, and searches for its food routing among the stones. It reaches a considerable size, being found in the Thames up to 12 lb and more.

145. *The Tench* prefers still waters and sluggish streams with muddy bottoms. In length, as a rule, it reaches 18 ins, but has been recorded up to 30 ins. *The Rough-tailed Stickleback* does not attain more than 3½ ins in length. As a rule it is an inland fish, but it also descends the rivers in shoals to the sea. *The Carp* thrives in ponds and slow running waters, spending the winter in the mud, and rising to the surface during the summer. It occasionally reaches 30 ins length.

The following Fisherman's Tables produced by H.T. Sheringham sum up the elusive nature of our quarry:

Carp Table
One day   = 18 hours
18 hours = 1 potato
10 years = 1 carp

Barbel Table
One swim = 3000 worms
One punt = 2 days
2 days   = 1 perch

Pike Table
One day   = 36 baits
One bait can = 3 men
36 baits   = 2 runs
2 runs   = 1 anecdote
1 anecdote   = 20 lb

Roach Table
19 feet   = 1 pole
3 pence   = 1 box of gentles
1 box of gentles = 300 chrysalises
300 chrysalises   = 1 public house
2 pints   = 1 crust
1 crust   = 2 fish
2 fish   = 9 oz
9 oz   = one plaied teapot

Salmon Table
1 holiday = 1 month
1 river   = £200
2 weeks   = 1 drought
4 floods   = 2 weeks
4 weeks   = 1 fish
1 fish   = 1 kelt*
1 kelt   = 1 fish†
1 angler   = 2 atheists

*Aberdeen reckoning
†London reckoning

under circumstances when anybody can take them, but who can conquer the most perplexing difficulties, and circumvent the most sharpened instincts – is a person of higher accomplishment and greater merit than an equally good salmon fisher.

Some consider salmon anglers too blasé. The following conversation recorded by H.T. Sheringham tends to confirm this:

A. So you're back. What's the news from the Fiskelv?
B. Poorish this year. Not enough snow. We only got – let me see *(consults notebook)*, yes, here it is – a hundred and two salmon and thirty-nine grilse. That's not much to two rods for Norway. It's not a good year if we don't reach two hundred all told.
A. Sea trout, too, I suppose.
B. Oh yes, sea trout, if you care about 'em. I don't, not on a salmon river. I don't mind a day or two with a small rod where there's nothing better to be had. What about you? Tay, as usual?
A. Yes, same old place. Same old story too. Seventy fish in the month. It's generally about that. Seven the best day. Jog-trot sport of course, but it suits me.
B. Anything big?
A. No, nothing over 29. Did you?
B. Let me see *(consults notebook again)*. Two over 40, and 5 over 30. Pretty fair, though we've done better with the big ones.

Many anglers become quite ecstatic when describing their quarry and understandably enthuse over the fish's appearance – its colours, size and shape. Pictures of fish are therefore popular with anglers and they adorn their walls and log books, etc. One can think of a number of angling writers who vividly describe their quarry, but I believe no one does it with more feeling than Zane Grey when he describes the dolphin, a sea fish not to be confused with the marine mammal of the same name:

My first sight of a dolphin near at hand was one to remember. The fish flashed gold – deep rich gold – with little flecks of blue and white. Then the very next flash there were greens and yellows – changing, colourful, brilliant bars. In that background of dark, clear, blue Gulf Stream water this dolphin was radiant, golden, exquisitely beautiful. It was a shame to lift him out of the water.

The appearance of the dolphin when just out of the water beggars description. Very few anglers in the world have ever had this experience. Not many anglers, perhaps, care for the beauty of a fish. But I do. And for the sake of those who feel the same way I wish I could paint him. But that seems impossible. For even while I gazed the fish changed colour. He should have been called the chameleon of the ocean. He looked a quivering, shimmering, changeful creature, the colour of golden-rod. He was the personification of beautiful colour alive. The fact that he was dying made the changing hues. It gave me a pang – that I should be the cause of the death of so beautiful a thing.

I, too, have caught dolphin, trolling off the coast of West Africa, and my feelings were very similar, but I could never have portrayed them so well.

146. An Edwardian postcard from Ste Anne de Bellevue,
Ontario, Canada, showing five Maskinonge or
Muskellinnge (Muskies) pike weighing 118 lb.

THE CATCH

Finally we come to our ultimate goal – the catch, our quarry successfully landed. Anglers have always had dreams of catching big fish or landing large numbers of fish as a climax to all their strivings and desires. It is not what we all go fishing for of course and not all of us want to catch large baskets of fish – well at least not regularly. There are some of us who would rather return fish surplus to our needs than go on killing for killing's sake, even though the advent of the deep-freeze has resolved the problem of what to do with the surplus catch. The coarse fisherman commendably returns his catch at the end of the day. He may photograph it of course and he may win money from it if he is a match angler, but he does return his quarry safely to the water alive. One reason which some give for his doing this is that his catch is inedible. However, anglers on the continent of Europe would disagree as they enjoy eating carp, roach, tench and the like.

Generally speaking we are more conservation-minded now, although there are still those who measure the pleasure of their day's fishing by the number of fish they catch. Records from the past speak for themselves and details of the size of many catches are enough to make some of us cringe. It is the catches of salmon and trout which tend to be the most accurately recorded. The works of Henderson, Stewart, Stoddart and Christopher North in Scotland have all recorded catching with monotonous regularity large baskets of trout. Their day's success was usually measured by the pannier-full and one Scots angler in the early nineteenth century notched up 312 trout averaging a quarter pound in one day's fishing – an outstanding 'haul', but catches in the three figures were not uncommon for a day's trout fishing in Scotland at that time. Catches of a similar magnitude were also recorded in England at that time: Ron Coleby, in his invaluable work *Regional Angling Literature*, refers to Professor John Wilson taking 324 trout, none of them above a pound, at Wastdalehead in May 1834.

Achievements with Atlantic salmon have probably been better documented than for any other fish. Some of the figures are mind-boggling. On the Grimersta river on the Isle of Lewis in 1888 a Mr A.M. Naylor caught 54 salmon in one day, totalling 314 lb; and he and two companions landed 333 salmon and 71 sea trout in six consecutive days. Certainly the conditions were unusual, as the river was experiencing an artificially induced spate during drought conditions at a time when large numbers of salmon were waiting in the sea for the drought to end. Such a catch does not go unparalleled. Rober Pashley, the 'wizard of the Wye', had many successful days and from 1897 to 1951 he caught 10,000 salmon including 29 over 40 lb. A detailed account of his achievements appear in *Wye Salmon and Other Fish* by J.A. Hutton and the second edition of the *Tale of a Wye Fisherman* by H.A. Gilbert.

147. The end of a happy day on an Irish (?) lough. The boat construction is Irish. Any guesses as to the locality?

Records of large catches of heavy salmon from the torrential rivers of Norway are equally staggering. Jack Chance in *Debrett's Salmon Stories* gives a fascinating breakdown of the Holkham Records of salmon taken from the Alta river in Norway by the Duke of Westminster and his friends between 1913 and 1929. One of their outstanding achievements occurred one July night when the Duke caught 33 salmon weighing 800 lb. Six of the fish were over 30 lb and two over 40 lb.

Another outstanding angler was Cyril Well who also fished in Norway, on the Bolstad river. Jack Chance gives a record of his catches and those of his guests: over a period of 207 weeks, fishing two rods, he and his friends caught 1496 salmon weighing 40,896 lb at an average weight of 27 lb.

The catches on some Canadian rivers are equally impressive. On the

148. One day's catch from the Big Falls Pool on the Humber River, Newfoundland, in the early 1920s. As the Falls were an obstacle to further ascent, fish used to accumulate in this pool and big catches were common. A good account of fishing this river is to be found in *A Little Fishing Book* by Cecil, Lord Harmsworth.

149. Some good rainbows from
Tarawera Lake, Rotorua, New Zealand.
A vintage postcard from the 1920s.

Cascapedia river Lord Lansdowne and his friends took large numbers of fish of a consistently high average weight. Probably the best day was in June 1879 when a Mr Ellis caught seventeen fish weighing 465 lb of which the individual weights were 38, 36, 36, 32, 32, 32, 32, 31, 30, 24, 24, 22, 22, 21, 21, 20 and 20 lb.

Further details of large catches of salmon would become monotonous. One is led to wonder what they did with all those fish in days when freezers were unheard of and the fishing lodges at which the anglers stayed were often miles from any other habitation – perhaps they smoked them. General Stewart, who fished for salmon in Iceland in the early part of this century, used to give his fish to the farmers in lieu of payment for the fishing.

A Morning Catch.

150. A pleasant picture depicting a morning catch of 'brookies'. This is an early (pre-1905) postcard from the States.

151

152

It is probably the 'monster' fish which the angler remembers most and which he catches again and again in his fireside dreams. More likely it is 'the one that got away' – the large india-rubber fish which grows in size each time the event is recalled. So often it is these lost 'monsters' which are remembered in idle moments when the incident is re-enacted but with the fish eventually being landed. Indeed, there is one consolation in losing a monster fish: its memory will stay with you longer than the one that you caught and ate. Chaytor, in his *Letters to a Salmon Fisher's Sons*, was sure that this was so:

But even success has its limits; the fish is caught, the thing is done. It is our lost fish that I believe stay longest in our memory, and seize upon our thoughts whenever we look back on fishing days. The most gallant fish

151. The catch in a Salmon Derby in Oregon, USA – seven salmon weighing 416 lb, including a tiddler of 45 lb.

152. A catch of sailfish from the waters around the Virgin Islands in the Caribbean.

153. A good catch of fish on the dam on Lake Winnibigoshish, Deer River, Minnesota.

154. A good day's sport, fishing camp on river bank, Florida. The biggest fish could be a Tarpon. A 1920 postcard with a postmark urging men to 'Join the Navy for training and travel'.

A Good Day's Sport, Fishing Camp on River Bank, Florida.

Salmon Fishing: A Twenty Pounder.

155. A twenty pounder from a Scottish salmon river. It could be the Spey, Dee or Tweed. A greenheart rod and a brass reel would suggest the period being early this century.

when eaten is forgotten, but the fish that, after a mad glorious battle, has beaten us and left us quivering with excitement and vexation, is hooked and lost again in many a year to come.

One can only imagine how Bishop Browne must have felt when, in the autumn of 1868, he hooked a huge Tay salmon near the mouth of the Earn and, after several hours extending into the night, it broke free when almost exhausted. Did he later in his dreams land the fish with the proffered lantern and gaff which he rejected at the time as taking unfair advantage of the fish?

Another large Scottish salmon lost in the final moments of the fight was hooked by Colonel Haig fishing the Tod Holes pool on the Tweed. It was lost at the net in the twilight, subsequently to be caught the same night in

156. A shark angling competition, Loo Cornwall.

a Cairn net. Its weight was estimated at being over 70 lb. But let Colonel Haig and the old porter at St Boswell's railway station have the last words:

'Yon was a gran' fish ye lost in the Tod Holes yon nicht sir.' 'Oh yeas' replied Colonel Haig. 'It was a good enough fish, but I never got a fair sight of him.' The porter stared at him solemnly. 'It was the biggest salmon that ever cam' oot o' the water o' Tweed.' 'How do you know that?' asked the astonished Laird. 'Fine I ken it,' said the porter. 'There was twae lads sittin' under the Wallace Monument forenent ye. They had a Cairn net wi' them, waiting for the darkenin'. They seen ye loss the fish, and they seen the wave o' him as he cam across the water. So they up and whuppit the net roon' him, and had himm oot. He was that big he wadna

157. A new British record – a Mako shark of 428½ lb, caught by Jack Sefton, Looe, Cornwall on 26 September 1961.

158. Another good shark, but this time from Egypt (postmark Cairo).

LOOE. 26 SEPT. 1961
MAKO 428½ LBS
NEW BRITISH RECORD
CAUGHT BY MR JACK SEFTON
BOAT "IRENE" SKIPPER RAY PENGELLY

MAKO SHARK

159. Leaping Tarpon caught at St Petersburg, Florida. A fascinating post-card posted in 1912. The weights of the largest fish are 148, 142 and 131 lb. This is an advertising card as a printed announcement on the back describes the release of a moving film of the Washington Birthday Parade by the makers Pathe-Freres Motion Picture Co which was available from the local film exchange. The writer has scribbled the message around the advert which says: 'The Mocking birds are busy here with their melodious songs.'

LEAPING TARPON, CAUGHT AT ST. PETERSBURG, FLA.
BY-THE-GULF-STREAM.

gang into the sack they had wi' them, so they cutit him in twae. They brocht the tae [tail] half to me to send awa' by the train, and the weight of that was five-and-thirty puns!'

A more unenviable loss was the monster Norwegian salmon hooked by Mr Bromley Davenport on the Rauma river. The sense of utter despair and amazement is conjured up by John Buchan in his account of the incident in *Great Hours in Sport*:

The fish was dead beat after a three hours struggle and a downstream battle of two miles. The experienced ghillie, who said it was the largest fish he had seen in his fifty years experience, was desperately nervous and made only bungling attempts to gaff it. The hold broke and, although the fish lay still on the surface, the man froze and made no attempt to land it.

SOME WORLD RECORDS
Here are record catches of six lake fish found in most Canadian waters. These game fish not only offer choice eating but provide a thrilling battle when hooked

MUSKELLUNGE – 69 LBS. 15 OZ.
LAKE TROUT – 63 LBS. 2 OZ.
SMALLMOUTH BASS – 11 LBS. 15 OZ.
LARGEMOUTH BASS – 22 LBS. 4 OZ.
WALLEYED PIKE – 25 LBS.
NORTHERN PIKE – 46 LBS. 2 OZ.

161

The poor angler in amazement wrested the gaff from the ghillie's hand but was just too late. The huge fins of the monster had begun to move and the salmon was slowly disappearing into the deep.

Mr Davenport's account captures the sense of loss with which we can sympathise:

But the fit passes, and a sorrow too deep for words gains possession of me, and I throw away the gaff and sit down, gazing in blank despair at the water. Is it possible? Is it not a hideous nightmare?

Another loss of such magnitude involves a carp in the disused ship canal at Ulverston, Lancashire. The large fish was hooked by Mr Till one hot afternoon in July 1917. After a long struggle he slowly drew it in and it lay lazily upon its side like a waterlogged boat. He edged the net down, reaching as far as he could, keeping the rod butt high behind him. And then, at the moment when he had that fish of his dreams almost dead at his

160. A contemporary Canadian post-card from Cranberry Portage, Manitoba, north of latitude '54. The caption on the reverse reads: 'Canada, with only 1% of the world's population, has over 15% of the world's fresh water surface. With hundreds of thousands of lakes being fed by countless miles of rivers and streams, it is truly an angler's paradise.'

161. A happy angler on the Morrumsa in Sweden with his catch of two large sea trout.

163. Trout fishing in the backwoods of Oregon. The fish are probably Cutthroat trout.

164. Where King Salmon Hit the Troll. This fisherman seems to use a handline on a wooden frame (top of picture) for trolling. The message on the back of the card simply says, 'Let's go fishing.'

feet, lying there flat and exhausted on the water, the gut gave and it slowly sank from view. His hands were shaking and he felt so sick with disappointment that he packed up and went home.

Such losses are probably only parallelled by one other, although fictitious. In this case Hemingway's Old Man caught his fish, a giant marlin, but it was subsequently lost to marauding sharks as he sailed home with his prize lashed to the side of his frail craft.

Thinking of marlin prompts me to include a loss of a swordfish recalled by Zane Grey:

'Look! Look!' I yelled to the above. 'Don't miss it! . . . Oh, great!'

'He's charging the boat!' hoarsely shouted Dan.

'He's all in!' yelled my brother.

I jumped into the cockpit and leaned over the gunwale beside the rod. Then I grasped the line, letting it slip through my hands. Dan wound in with fierce energy. I felt the end of the double line go by me, and at this I

162. A recent card showing salmon from the Grand Cascapedia, Quebec, Canada.

TROUT FISHING, OREGON.

11710.   Where King Salmon Hit the Troll.
Published by W. H. Case, Juneau, Alaska.

12. A MORNINGS CATCH OF SPECKLED TROUT.
BLACK HILLS, S. D.
COPYRIGHTED 1911 BY W. B. PERKINS.

This time the big one
didn't get away
22 Pound Lake Trout
CASPIAN LAKE
GREENSBORO, VT.

Richardson
1302

let out another shout to warn Dan. Then I had the end of the leader – a good strong grip – and, looking down, I saw the clear silver outline of the hugest fish I had ever seen short of shark or whale. He made a beautiful, wild, frightful sight. He rolled on his back. Roundbill or broadbill, he had an enormous length of sword.

'Come, Dan – we've got him' I panted. Dan could not, dare not get up then.

The situation was perilous. I saw how Dan clutched the reel, with his big thumbs biting into the line. I did my best. My sight failed for an instant. But the fish pulled the leader through my hands. My brother leaped down to help – alas, too late!

'Let go Dan! Give him line!'

But Dan was past that. Afterward he said his grip was locked. He held,

165. A morning's catch of speckled trout, Black Hills, South Dakota. The caption on the reverse of this 1911 card says: 'The streams of the Black Hills are now well-stocked with Rainbow, Brook and Mountain Trout. You are invited to join us in this grand spot.'

166. A young angler with a 22 lb Lake Trout from Caspian Lake, Greensboro, Vermont.

CAMPING IN THE WOODS OF MAINE. 6. 106295

167. Camping in the woods of Maine. A nice catch of trout ready for the log fire. The large panniers are canoe baskets which keep belongings dry while on the water. Posted in Portland, Maine, in 1929.

168. An old card from Maine handed out with the compliments of Maine Central Railroad. The reverse side of the card has an undivided back and only space for the address which indicates that the card was possibly printed prior to 1906. The divided back, providing space for a message, was introduced on British cards in 1902, but two or three years later in other countries.

169. A nice bag of tench (top), seventeen bream and two roach. The figure for the total weight is not completely printed, but we are told that the fish were caught on Raby's famous hooks on 8 August 1931.

and not another foot did the swordfish get. Again I leaned over the gunwale. I saw him – a monster – pale, wavering. His tail had an enormous spread. I could no longer see his sword. Almost he was ready to give up.

Then the double line snapped. I fell back in the boat and Dan fell back in the chair.

Nine hours!

There is some consolation in the loss of a monster fish to be found in William Humphry's *My Moby Dick* which describes the relationship he had with a gigantic one-eyed trout. The first few lines follow:

Even so worldly a man as Jonathan Swift could write in later life, in a letter to his friend Alexander Pope, 'I remember when I was a little boy, I felt a great fish at the end of my line, which I drew up almost to the ground, but it dropped in, and the disappointment vexes me to this day.' Sick with disappointment at losing my once-in-lifetime fish, I was sure I would never get over it.

But now I wonder, would I really rather have that fish, or a plastic replica of him, hanging on my wall than to see him as I do in my memory, flaunting his might and his majesty against the rainbow of his own making?

The angler's catch figures significantly in angling competitions. These can be big events involving several hundred anglers lined or 'staked out' at pegs along the river banks. Strict rules are laid down and religiously observed. The winner is often rewarded with a monetary prize frequently reaching four figures. Angling matches are not the sole right of coarse fishermen, although they, probably more than any other class of angler, participate in this type of fishing most frequently. Trout anglers,

The kind of Square
Tail Brook Trout they
catch in Maine.
Send for book telling
all about it. Address,
F. E. Boothby, General
Passenger Agent, Maine
Central Railroad, Port-
land, Me.

lbs. Caught on Rabt's Famous Hooks. Aug 8th - 1931.

170. Two youngsters with a fine catch of Albacore at Redondo Beach, California. Posted at Redondo in 1912.

particularly in Scotland, also hold fishing competitions and have indulged in them since at least the latter part of the last century. These events are usually held on such waters as Loch Leven where the International Championship with England, Ireland and Wales takes place. Angling contests are also held in other parts of Scotland and on the Border rivers clubs have held these events annually for many years, with valuable trophies being presented to the winners at the club dinners. Sea anglers, too, have their carnivals and festivals and in this branch of angling the holiday angler has just as much chance of success as the expert. I have never heard of a salmon angling competition in this country, although salmon 'Derbies' are held at various resorts along the Pacific coast of the United States. Perhaps one day angling will be a recognised event in the Olympic Games and there will be 'golds' awarded to the angler catching the greatest number of fish and the largest; and similar awards for those who can demonstrate their prowess in casting.

Not all anglers approve of fishing competitions as it detracts from the true nature of angling. In some trout clubs rigid rules are laid down regarding fishing competition procedures which suggest that malpractice is suspected, and expected, among the participants, and that 'trust' goes unrecognised in their competitions. It is quite easy to debase the sport and destroy its traditional associations with quietness, relaxation and opportunity to think. As Roderick Haig-Brown remarked, when considering this aspect of fishing:

Angling is not a competitive sport. The fisherman's only real competition is with his quarry and his only real challenge is the challenge to himself. Nothing can add to this, but the height of interhuman competition can certainly detract from it. There are casual forms of competition that are relatively harmless, such as a side bet between friends or the affectionate regard for fish of record size taken on tackle of closely defined specifications or the many types of local club awards that have more to do with good fellowship than competition. But there is little good to be said for the so-called fish derbies, which are nearly always directed to commercial ends by tourism entrepreneurs and advertisers of all kinds. At best they are a perversion of the real nature of the sport; at worst they can be seriously damaging to the resource itself.

One does not have to enter angling competitions to win prizes. In recent years a number of firms have given generously to any angler catching the largest fish of various types each month. The makers of a certain brand of sherry started the fashion many years ago by donating a bottle of their product to the captor of any trout over 4 lb in weight caught on fly. However, it is Ballantine's, the famous Scotch Whisky distillers, who offer the most to anglers catching the largest salmon, sea trout, brown trout and rainbow trout on fly each month of the fishing season, as it is not only the winner who is rewarded, but also several runners-up, and after that there are also consolation prizes, in the form of varying amounts of their product!

The desire for large catches of fish, monster fish and to win competitions above all else is not, however, a true measure of an angler. John Younger, the St Boswell shoemaker, said in his *River Angling for Salmon and Trout* that 'a man is never a master angler so long as a desire to have his hooked fish to land excites in his feelings the least agitation'. Angling is a leisurely art and we should pursue it as such. In his previously quoted article in *The Gentleman's Magazine* in 1893, entitled 'Angling in Still Waters', John Buchan remarked that:

To some men angling comes as a pleasure, to others as a business, and to others as a toil. Some men, notably those who have been poachers in their youth, can be seen sallying forth morning after morning, at an appointed time, with the usual paraphernalia of the fishermen. They go home at night, worn out with their exertions, only to renew them on the next day. Such men have no soul above their catch; if they make an especially large basket their spirits will be exuberant for a week; times and seasons are

171. A postcard from Eastman's Studio showing a neatly arranged catch of trout. Ideal for the angler who wishes to send home a photo-ready picture of his catch, although not every angler will manage to catch three brown trout with a total weight of 21 lb!

172. A catch of crappies and perch from Elephant Butte Dam near Hot Springs, New Mexico.

remembered only in connection with some piscatorial exploit . . . The experienced angler, always provided that he has gained his knowledge by personal experience and not from books, is a companion fit for the gods.

Certainly most of us will agree with the old countryman's remark in this article when he enquired after the day's success of the anglers: 'Aweel, if ye hadna' gotten ony ye would aye have had the graun' scenery.'

After all, that is what fishing is all about. It is only the Philistine who expects results from a day's work, be it only the achievement of so many holes at golf, so many sets of lawn tennis, or so many mph in a car. He cannot understand that a day's enjoyment is not to be measured in the weight of fish.

A Five-Ton Catch of Albacore, with Rod and Reel
Santa Catalina Island, Cal.

173. A five-ton catch of albacore with rod and reel, Santa
Catalina Island, California. Such catches were common-
place in the early part of this century, but as Zane Grey
said: 'The Japs, the Austrians, the round-haul nets, the
canneries and fertilizer plants, greed and war has cast their
dark shadow over this beautiful area.' By 1918 the albacore
fishing was poor, attributed to overfishing and the exploita-
tion of the local kelp beds in which the fish spawned.

REFLECTIONS

Now is the time to sit and reflect and contemplate on the future of fishing. The previous chapters have shown how, over the years, so many of us have enjoyed our sport. A sport which, for many, involves a complete and life-long dedication. Many come to fishing early in life while others join the pilgrimage in later years. Those of us who frequented streams and lakes from early childhood equipped with makeshift fishing tackle will have unrivalled memories of happy hours, perhaps in the company of others of our own age or with parents or mentors who brought to us an awareness of the living world. This is often only gained at an impressionable time in our young lives and is difficult to acquire in later life. To me the early memories of fish caught are less vivid than the memories of my companions, surroundings and fish lost. Some would say then that I could have gained these impressions without going fishing, but simply by being by the waterside. What a futile form of reasoning that is but, alas, it is one that is being advanced by the anti-blood sports fraternity whose main aim in life is to stop people enjoying themselves.

Angling surveys mentioned earlier in this book show how rapidly the recruitment to the army of anglers is rising. However, as Roderick Haig-Brown pointed out in his book *Bright Waters, Bright Fish*:

One difficulty with surveys is that they probably tend to reflect the casual or marginal angler too heavily – that is the man, woman or child who fishes because it seems to be part of a holiday. This individual and his or her preferences are undoubtedly important to the tourist industry, but they have no validity whatsoever in terms of what sport fishing is all about. The marginal fisherman may be going in either of two directions – right out of the sport altogether or more deeply into it. If the former, there is not much need to worry about him – some other form of recreation will probably claim his attention. But if it is the latter, and especially if he is young, his preferences should be carefully examined,

Daily more round-about,
Hourly more plump and stout,
No wonder Poor Miss Trout,
    Fears those bad hooks.

Artfully, Skinny Sprat,
Sells her his Anti-fat,
Saying that only that
    Saves from the hooks.

Old Dr. Gudgeon kept a School,
  A most select affair;
He taught the little fishes sums
  And of all bait beware.

174

because angling needs likely recruits in every generation and there can be no doubt that a deep interest in angling will be of value to him all through his life.

I think it is fair to say though that, even taking the holiday angler into account, the army of dedicated anglers is growing steadily. One might agree that, with a rising number of anglers and considering the number of fish an angler can catch in a day, the loss inflicted on our fish populations could get out of hand. Roderick Haig-Brown responds to this allegation most sensibly when he says:

The mature fisherman . . . is likely to answer the philosophical question 'Why go fishing?' with his senses rather than with positive thought: I, this human entity, gain immensely more than any loss I am inflicting. The fisherman who articulates an answer to the question may add: I am using the resource carefully, well within its capacity to maintain itself. I am learning more about it and its meaning. Without my concern and interest, self-centred though they be, in all probability the resource would be entirely destroyed by some other human activity.

As I said in an early chapter, the angler, being aware of his environment, is quick to detect undesirable change and can alert the authorities when pollution occurs and can pressurise industry to reduce its effluents.

It must be borne in mind that angling is a sport and the word 'sport', in any connotation, implies a sense of generosity towards the opponent, a desire to meet and test honourably under conditions fair enough to ensure that the outcome is uncertain. As Roderick Haig-Brown points out:

If these implications are lost or destroyed the meaning of sport

174, 175. Two postcards (one with a 1904 postmark) on a 'warning to fish' theme, where fish warn fish of the danger of hooks and bait.

disappears. In athletic sports the ideal is often lost for commercial or competitive reasons. In field sports, such as fishing, there is no sense or reason in losing the ideal, since the sportsman is at most testing himself and that not too earnestly if he understands his sport properly.

Angling, if it is to persist, can only do so as a sport of high principles, strong ethics and intelligent recognition of the true nature of the resource. Such principles, like the ordinary concrete regulations that bind him under law, are not a burden upon the angler but positive enhancement of his chosen pursuit. To be fit to make proper use of the fishing, he has to bring something more with him than a rod, a line, a hook and a desire to kill fish.

There are, of course, the usual enforceable regulations which the angler has to observe. Many of these are laid down by law while others are set by individual angling associations or clubs. These enforceable regulations include fishing seasons, gear restrictions, methods of fishing and size and bag limits. Unfortunately many of the more undesirable effects of angling, which can result from lack of thought or care, are those least enforceable and are the ones for which the angler is criticised most strongly. These include maltreatment of fish, destruction of the waterside environment and the effects on wildlife from disturbance, discarded nylon and lead shot.

The general public frequently sums up the standard of the sport by the conduct of its participants. As we have seen, anglers were considered to be patient, contemplative men who communed with nature, but the impact on the non-angling public of the following headlines from the weekly angling papers must be one of incredulity: 'Barbel riot at Bewdley'; 'Pike Teach-in'; 'Crucian Cracker'; 'Ton-up Tench Catch'; and 'Family Bream Bash'. A headline such as 'Louts and Hypocrites — they are the anglers I detest' can only generate bewilderment.

176. Although this Valentine's card was posted in 1908, its sentiments are most topical today and many would not agree with the remarks on the card: 'When you get a bite pull for all you're worth, never mind what other fellows tell you about "playing your fish" – you are here for business not playing.'

Certainly the excessive use of the waterside by anglers in groups has, whether along a reservoir or river, resulted in complaints from landowners and dismay from other water users. The lighting of fires is a common practice, particularly among night-fishers, and the dangers from such actions are obvious. Litter is another perennial problem and recently the London Anglers' Association bailiffs filled ninety large plastic bags with litter from the banks of the Grand Union Canal between Watford and Tring. They also found no less than forty bank sticks or 'idle jacks'. The Association has now introduced a £50 litter fine and the Birmingham Anglers' Association is also making intensive efforts to overcome the ever-growing problem. To be fair to the anglers this rubbish is often produced by large bank-trampling audiences which attend match-angling contests.

The following extract from a sea angler's letter to an angling newspaper is a good guide to the feelings of some anglers to their fellow 'sportsmen' when they infringed the normal code of good conduct both to man and to fish:

After fishing for an hour and catching over 100 fish, I packed up and walked along the pier and never have I seen such a disgusting, deplorable sight in my life. Anglers were throwing fish against the wall to kill them, gutting fish on the wall and path and throwing discarded heads and guts into the railway wagons and railway yards below . . . Anglers were also taking baggage trolleys from the station to carry their hundreds of fish home.

Fortunately this type of incident is rare, but it is one that critics would use in their fight against angling. A *Code of Practice for Handling Fish* was drawn up by the National Federation of Anglers, the Salmon and Trout Association and the National Federation of Sea Anglers and has been produced by the National Anglers' Council. If all anglers were to observe this code there could be no adverse criticism. Similar codes have also been prepared in other countries, and the International Atlantic Salmon Foundation in North America issued simple instructions for releasing salmon unharmed.

Zane Grey had this attitude to fishing over sixty-five years ago and had this to say in one of this books:

I have demonstrated the practicability of letting Marlin swordfish go after they were beaten, but almost all of the boatmen will not do it. The greater number of swordfish weigh under two hundred pounds, and when exhausted and pulled up to the boat they can be freed by cutting the wire leader close to the hook. Probably all these fish will live. A fisherman will have his fun seeing and photographing the wonderful leaps, and conquering the fish, and when all this is over it would be sportsmanlike to let him go.

However, one's quarry must not be too exhausted so that when it is released it is too weak to recover and eventually dies. These anglers that nowadays advocate light lines to catch heavy fish should heed this warning. Many years ago Zane Grey was well aware of this and it is surprising that more anglers do not realise this. As Zane Grey says:

Brutal it is to haul in a fish on tackle so heavy that he has no chance for his life; likewise it is brutal to hook a fish on tackle so light that, if he does not

177. Watching fish, whether leaping falls or swimming in pools, gives many people a great deal of pleasure. The Fairy Springs Trout Pool, Rotorua, New Zealand.

178. The roles reversed! How would you like it if . . .? Postmark 1939.

break it, he must be followed around and all over, chased by a motorboat hour after hour, until he practically dies of exhaustion.

Other less familiar modifications to traditional regulations are happily creeping into our sport with a view to protecting, and respecting, our quarry. They include protected areas, 'catch-and-release', the use of single barbless hooks and more realistic bag limits. In the United States, to promote catch-and-release fishing, various authorities have established what are known as Lunker Release Award Programs. Anglers who release 18 inch or larger trout receive a patch for their fishing jacket which features the trout park name, thus: 'I released a Lunker at Bennett Spring.' Similar patches are issued for releasing Atlantic salmon in Canada. In Austria there are some stretches of river where one is compelled to return all fish caught, while on other waters the bag limit is restricted to two fish a day.

In both Germany and Austria there are certain areas of a lake or sections of a river where fishing is forbidden. These prohibited areas are usually spawning grounds. Furthermore, in Germany all anglers have to pass an exam before being issued with a licence to fish. The exam is in the form of sixty multiple-choice questions covering fish anatomy and morphology, disease, freshwater ecology and law. Although such regimentation is not necessarily a good thing it does give the anglers a sense of responsibility for their natural heritage, and perhaps a gentle education of would-be anglers in this country would be a good thing. The issue of a *Code of Practice for Anglers* with the water authority licence, or in Scotland with a fishing ticket, might serve the same purpose as the issue of *The Highway Code* with a provisional car licence. So much for the lecture, but finally take note of the words written by Richard Brookes in 1766:

Remember that the Wit and Invention of Mankind were bestowed for other Purposes than to deceive silly Fish; and that however delightful Angling may be, it ceases to be innocent when used otherwise than as a mere Recreation.

BIBLIOGRAPHY

Anon., *Angling in Britain*. Report of the Travis Commission. Angling Foundation, 1980.

Anon., Report of the Panel of Enquiry into Shooting and Angling (1976-1979). Horsham: R.S.P.C.A., 1982

Buchan, John, *Scholar Gipsies*. London: John Lane, The Bodley Head, 1896.

Buchan, John, (Ed.), *Great Hours in Sport*. London and Edinburgh: Nelson.

Burnand, F.C., *The Incompleat Angler*. London: Bradbury, Agnew & Co, 1887.

Chance, Jack, *Debrett's Salmon Stories*. London: Debrett's Peerage, 1983.

Chaytor, A.U., *Letters to a Salmon Fisher's Sons*. London: John Murray, 1910.

Coleby, R.J.W., *Regional Angling Literature*. Lincoln: Coleby, 1979.

Farson, Negley, *Going Fishing*. London: Country Life, 1942.

Fedden, Romilly, *Golden Days*. London: A. & C. Black, 1919.

Grey, Zane, *Tales of Fishes*. Hodder & Stoughton.

Haig-Brown, Roderick, *Bright Waters, Bright Fish*. Vancouver: Douglas and McIntyre, 1980.

Harmsworth, Lord Cecil, *A Little Fishing Book*. London: Frederick Muller, 1942.

Hemingway, Ernest, *The Old Man and the Sea*. London: Jonathan Cape, 1952.

Holt, Tonie and Valmai, *Picture Postcards of the Golden Age: A Collector's Guide*. London: Postcard Publishing Company, 1978.

Humphry, William, *My Moby Dick*. Chatto & Windus, 1979.

Lockhart, Robert Bruce, *My Rod, My Comfort*. London: Putnam, 1957.

McCaskie, Norman, *Fishing, My Life's Hobby*. London: Falcon Press, 1950.

MacDonald, John, *The Origins of Angling*. New York: Doubleday, 1963.

Radcliffe, William, *Fishing from the Earliest Times*. London: John Murray, 1921.

Ransome, Arthur, *Rod and Line*. London: Jonathan Cape, 1929.

Sheringham, H.T., *Fishing: Its Cause, Treatment and Cure*. London: Philip Allan, 1925.

Walton, Izaak, *The Compleat Angler*, 1653. Gallienne Edition (1897) London: John Lane, The Bodley Head.

Younger, John, *River Angling for Salmon and Trout*. Kelso: Rutherford, 1864.

INDEX

of Card Publishers

41. Publisher not known
42. Iles, Rotorua, New Zealand
43. Publisher not known
44. Utgefandi: Photosport, Reykjavik, Iceland
45. Utgefandi: Photosport, Reykjavik, Iceland
46-48. Valentine & Sons Publishing Co Ltd, New York. Artotype series
49. Iles, Rotorua, New Zealand
50. Lawson Graphics Atlantic, Canada
51. The Cochrane Co, Palatka, Florida, USA
52. C.M. Corrington's International Novelty & Art Co, St Louis, Mo, USA
53. Publisher not known; artist R.H. Ramilly
54. Publisher not known
55. Smith-Western Inc, USA
56. Raphael Tuck & Sons, 'Oilette'
57. Langsdorff & Co, London; artist M. Morris
58. British series
59-60. Raphael Tuck & Sons. Connoisseur series
61. Raphael Tuck & Sons, 'Oilette'
62-66. G. D. & D., London; artist H.C. Earnshaw. Star series
67-69. Publisher not known
70. Publisher not known; artist F. Macleod
71. E.C. Kropp Co, Milwaukee, USA
72. Freak Fish series
73-74. Publisher not known
75-78. Publisher not known
79. Publisher not known
80. Arthur Guinness & Sons Plc
81. Valentine's of Dundee Ltd
82. The Frank Swallow Post Card Co Inc, USA
83. J.C. Breaden
84. Mike Roberts, Berkeley, USA
85. Valentine & Sons, London and Dublin; Bonzo series
86. Litbra H.F., Reykjavik, Iceland
87. Curteichcolor ® 3-D Natural Colour Reproduction, USA
88. Felix McGlennon Ltd, London. View series
89. P.H.
90. H.B. Series, London; artist Donald McGill
91. Raphael Tuck & Sons; artist Lance Thackeray
92. Raphael Tuck & Sons, 'Oilette'; artist Ellam
93. Hartmann; artist D. Hardy. Sporting Girls series

140-145. Raphael Tuck & Sons, 'Aquarette'; artist R.J. Wealthy. British Freshwater
    Fish series
146. Canadian Grand Trunk Railway System
147. Publisher not known
148. J.C. Parsons, Corner Brook, Newfoundland
149. Iles, Rotorua, New Zealand
150. Hugh C Leighton Co, Portland, Maine, USA
151. Noko, USA
152. The Art Shop, St Thomas, Virgin Islands
153. Lakeland Colour Press, Brainerd, Minnesota, USA
154. H. &. W.B. Drew Co, Jacksonville, Florida, USA. Florida Artistic series
155. Raphael Tuck & Sons. British Sports series
156. A.E. Raddy & Son, Looe, Cornwall
157. Jack's Photographic Service
158. Publisher not known
159. A.B. Archibald, St Petersburg, Florida, USA
160. Alex Wilson Coldstream Ltd, Dryden, Ontario, Canada
161. Forlag: Kungsforskiosken, Mörrum, Sweden
162. Publisher not known
163. Publisher not known
164. W.H. Case, Juneau, Alaska, USA
165. L.B. Hollister, South Dakota, USA
166. Publisher not known
167. Publisher not known
168. Maine Central Railroad, USA
169. Publisher not known
170. Newman Postcard Co, Los Angeles and San Francisco, USA
171. Eastman's Studios, USA
172. Flasher's Inc, Pomona, California, USA
173. Newman Postcard Co, Los Angeles and San Francisco, USA
174-175. Publisher not known
176. Valentine's of Dundee Ltd
177. Colin Branch Wholesale, Rotorua, New Zealand
178. Curt Teich Inc, Chicago, USA